KT-130-646

Sustainable Consumer Services

Business Solutions for Household Markets

Minna Halme, Gabriele Hrauda, Christine Jasch, Jaap Kortman, Helga Jonuschat, Michael Scharp, Daniela Velte and Paula Trindade

EARTHSCAN

London • Sterling, VA

83218

First published by Earthscan in the UK and USA in 2005

Copyright © Minna Halme, 2005

All rights reserved

ISBN-13:   978-1-844072-09-5   hardback
ISBN-10:   1-84407-209-6   hardback

Typesetting by Michael Scharp
Printed and bound in the UK by Cromwell Press, Trowbridge

Cover design by Adrian Senior
Cover photos by Art & Design City Helsinki, Motiva Ltd, Mika Kanerva and
Kari Mononen

For a full list of publications please contact:

Earthscan
8–12 Camden High Street
London, NW1 0JH, UK
Tel: +44 (0)20 7387 8558
Fax: +44 (0)20 7387 8998
Email: earthinfo@earthscan.co.uk
Web: **www.earthscan.co.uk**

22883 Quicksilver Drive, Sterling, VA 20166-2012, USA

Earthscan is an imprint of James & James (Science Publishers) Ltd and
publishes in association with the International Institute for Environment and
Development

A catalogue record for this book is available from the British Library

Library of Congress Cataloging-in-Publication Data has been applied for

Printed on elemental chlorine-free paper

The Library
University College for the Creative Arts
at Epsom and Farnham

338.
761
333
72
SUS

Contents

Preface

This book is based on a European research project called *Homeservice: Benchmarking Sustainable Services for the City of Tomorrow*. The motivation underlying the project was to discover why eco-efficient consumer services were not more popular among users, even though they could fulfil the same needs as products while replacing more material- and energy-intensive forms of consumption. More importantly, what could be done to make eco-efficient service based consumption models more attractive? These were the guiding questions with which the Sustainable Homeservice team started out in September 2002. They date back to 1999, when we wrote the first words of the homeservice project plan. The questions stemmed from a number of previous European and national research projects in which we had been involved: *Eco-Services, Dematerialization: the potential of services and ICT* and *sustainable homeservice* projects in Germany and Austria, to name a few, and some other scientific and practical observations.

Over the following years these questions became more and more pronounced when it turned out that in consumer markets, it was extremely challenging for eco-efficient services to win ground from ever-increasing product consumption. Some findings indicated that one of the preconditions for the realization of eco-efficiency promises was that consumers should be able to use such services as easily or conveniently as the products they own themselves. We then decided to study services that are offered to consumers at their homes. Based on this idea, we coined the term 'sustainable homeservice' to refer to services that are offered to consumers at their home and contribute positively to sustainable development in its environmental, social and economic dimensions.

For two years we studied the sustainability potential of services provided to households directly at their dwelling or on the premises. The project was carried out in six European countries – Austria, Finland, Germany, the Netherlands, Portugal and Spain. This book is one of the outcomes of the research project, and therefore most of the evidence is from these six countries.

What are the household services in this book about? In essence they are services that relate to and support our everyday lives. A large part of the services studied are relatively simple concepts. They are social rather than technological innovations, although creative use of ICT is characteristic to a number of the best examples. About 20 services are described in detail in the book, but altogether over 200 sustainable homeservices serve as the background evidence. The ones that are not described in the book can be explored at www.sustainable-homeservices.com.

This book will give answers to the questions phrased above. It will even give instructions for designing sustainable household services, yet it is not a cookbook. Such services and their provision frameworks are so context-dependent that it would not make sense to write a detailed recipe, because different international environments call for somewhat different service concepts. Hence the book is best utilized as a source of ideas for and experiences of innovative homeservice provision and use.

We owe thanks to several people who joined us in different parts of the research process behind this book. There were more people in the research team than the eight of us whose names appear in the list of authors. Thank you, Markku Anttonen, Johannes Puhrer, Cristina Rocha, Raquel Serrano, Erica Derijcke, Ibon Zugasti, Paula Duarte, Rui Fernandes, David Camocho, Joost Gijswijt, Ulrike Schöflinger, Franz Horvath, Sabine Kranzl and Irune Elorduy! In addition, Eva Heiskanen and Mikko Jalas have given insightful comments all along the way. We are indebted to Eva also for language editing. Oksana Mont's work and discussions with her have been helpful, too. We also benefited from the feedback of the reviewers of *Ecological*

Economics and the *Journal of Cleaner Production*, in which part of this work has been reported.

This study would not have been possible without financing from the European Commission. We are grateful to "The City of Tomorrow and Cultural Heritage" programme and Research Directorate-General (H). Vincent Favrel from the EU deserves a special mention for seeing the practical value of the findings and proposing to make a DVD film of the service examples in order to communicate the message to a wider audience. The film eventually became two films, a 15- and a 30-minute version. They are available in English and German and can be requested from info@ioew.at or halme@hkkk.fi.

We would also like to thank many people from different organizations that gave us their time and helped us to understand the reality of household service provision from many different angles. These services are very varied and they are provided by several constituencies from the public sector, housing organizations and NGOs to business enterprises. Here we would like to especially name a few housing organizations for good homeservice examples that showed us that it is possible to offer innovative everyday services that make the lives of residents a bit nicer and produce environmental benefits while doing that. These are: VVO, Gemeinnützige Siedlungs- und Wohnungsbaugesellschaft Berlin, Genossenschaft Bremer Höhe eG, Lekker Leven, the Roihuvuori and Maunula units of the City of Helsinki housing company, and Hübl & Partner. We would also like to thank several private and public sector representatives in Bilbao for participating in focus group discussions. Finally, thanks to Leopold Bernhard and all the others who have cooperated with us in making the DVD.

For some of us, parts of the research process for this book were personally very engaging. We would like to thank our near ones for their patience with sometimes exceptionally absent-minded family members.

The authors

Dr. Minna Halme is an adjunct professor at the Helsinki School of Economics and a senior research fellow at the Academy of Finland. She is a member of the editorial board of *Business Strategy and the Environment*, the Action Planning Committee of the *Greening of the Industry Network* and the administrative board of *WWF Finland*. Her areas of expertise include: sustainable services, business models for sustainable development, environmental corporate cultures, environmental communication and sustainability networks. Dr. Halme has published in several scientific journals including: *Ecological Economics, Journal of Management Studies, Business Strategy and the Environment, Scandinavian Journal of Management, Business Ethics Quarterly, Greener Management International, Business Ethics: A European Review, Journal of Cleaner Production,* and *The Finnish Journal of Business Economics.* Since 1992, she has been teaching corporate environmental management on Master's degree, executive MBA and doctoral courses in Finland and internationally.

Dr. Gabriele Hrauda is a freelance biologist, working since more than 10 years in close cooperation with the IÖW in Vienna. In the early 90s the main fields of interest were eco-balances, life-cycle assessment, waste management concepts and pollution prevention projects, like the PREPARE Project. Recently her focus in the field of ecological economics has changed to research on sustainable development, particularly eco-design and the creation and implementation of sustainable services. She is also involved in environmental teaching and nature interpretation, including lectures, workshops, post-graduate courses and outdoor training activities covering various biological and ecological topics.

Dr. Christine Jasch is the director of the Institute for Environmental Management and Economics, IÖW Austria. She is also a certified public accountant and a verifier for EMAS, ISO 14001 and sustainability reports. She serves as the Austrian delegate of ISO TC 207 and the Sustainability Working Party of the *Federation des Experts Comptables Européens* (FEE) in Brussels and is the chairperson of the equivalent Austrian bodies. She holds a membership in the expert working group on EMA of UN DSD. Her current working areas include environmental performance evaluation and sustainability indicators, integrated management systems, environmental and sustainability accounting, ethical investment, sustainability reporting, sustainable household services and product-service systems.

Mr. Jaap Kortman is a member of the management team of IVAM research and consultancy on sustainability, University of Amsterdam, the Netherlands. He is the manager of the departments Sustainable Building and Chain Management. For the department of Chain Management he has been analysing the environmental potential of services and product-service system in three European projects: Ecoservices, Homeservices and Chemical Product Services. He is responsible for the development of computer tools for the assessments of the sustainable performance of services. He is member of the international Task group Urban Sustainability (Tg38) of the International Council for Research and Innovation in Building and Construction.

Helga Jonuschat holds a master's degree in architecture and urban planning. She works as a scientific assistant at the IZT– Institute for Futures Studies and Technology Assessment, Berlin, since 2000. Her research focuses on sustainable urban and regional development, the city and region of the future, and ICT applications for the housing sector and homeservices. She is currently preparing her PhD thesis on social networks in the information age.

Dr. Michael Scharp works as a project manager at IZT, the Institute for Futures Studies and Technology Assessment. He holds a Ph.D in chemistry and a master's degree in philosophy. His current working areas are methods of innovation transfer: benchmarking, service engineering, sustainable housing und building and environmental education. Dr. Scharp has published in several German housing journals like *Die Wohnungswirtschaft*, *Taschenbuch für den Wohnungswirt* and *Bundesbaublatt*. He lectures on sustainable housing, services of housing organisations and service engineering. He also works together with the real estate associations like Berlin-Brandenburgischer Wohnungsverband and Bundesverband deutscher Wohnungsunternehmen in Germany and is a member of the advisory board of the Gewog – Gemeinützige Wohnungsbaugesellschaft Kleinmachnow gmbH.

Daniela Velte is partner and senior researcher at Prospektiker European Institute for Futures Studies and Strategic Planning in the Basque Country, Spain. She studied translation and economics at the University of Heidelberg and lived for one year in New York before settling down in Spain. Her current work areas include energy and environmental research, especially related to futures studies. She is also in charge of managing multiple European research projects in which Prospektiker participates.

Paula Trindade has a degree in chemistry from the University of Lisbon. Since 1995 she has been a researcher at the Centre for Sustainable Business Development of INETI (National Institute of Engineering, Technology and Innovation) in the areas of cleaner production, eco-efficiency and wastewater treatment. At present her work focuses on sustainable services, integrated product policy (IPP) and green procurement. She is involved in several European projects and coordinates one major LIFE Environment project in the area of IPP.

List of figures

List of tables

List of acronyms and abbreviations

ASDL	Fast internet connection
BDBN	Buenos Dias/Buenas Noches, a Spanish homeservice intermediary
CSD	Commission on Sustainable Development
ELIAS	Intermediary service for homeservices operating in the internet, Finland
EPA	Energy performance advice
EU	European Union
EuP	European Union's directive on energy using products
GNP	Gross national product
GSW	Gemeinnützige Siedlungs- und Wohnungsbaugesellschaft Berlin mbH, a German social housing company
HDI	Human development index
HO	Housing organisation
ICT	Information and communication technologies
ISEW	Index of sustainable economic welfare
MA	Magistratsabteilung
na	not available

NPO	Non-profit organisation
NU	Sustainable incentive card scheme in Rotterdam, The Netherlands
OECD	Organisation for Economic Cooperation and Development
QFM	Quality function management
R.U.S.Z	Reparatur- und ServiceZentrum, an Austrian social enterprise focusing on collection and repair of electronic appliances
SWOT	strength, weakness, opportunities and threats (method)
T&T	Työ & Toiminta ry, a Finnish social enterprise
TTS	Työtehoseura, Finnish Work Efficiency Institute
TV	Television
UNDP	United Nations Development Programme
UNEP	United Nations Environment Programme
VIVAGO	ICT-based wrist care system, a personal health monitoring appliance combined with a care service
VVO	A Finnish social housing company
WBG	Wohnungsbaugesellschaft Mahrzahn, a German social housing company
WCED	The World Commission on Environment and Development
WEEE	European Union's directive on waste of electronic and electrical equipment

1 Win-win-win? Ecologically, socially and economically sound services

During the recent decade, services have been acknowledged as one of the most prominent solutions to reduce the material and energy intensity of consumption, and thus put a halt to one of the main sources of environmental degradation. Despite the high hopes placed on eco-efficient services, they have mainly not made such a great success among consumers as their proponents expected. Why not? What could be done to make eco-efficient service-based consumption and lifestyles more attractive among consumers?

This book is about services that are offered to consumers at their homes and affect sustainable development positively in its ecological, social and economic dimensions. It seeks to unravel some of the blind spots of sustainable consumer services, and thereby build the ground for more successful future service solutions. We ask what kinds of consumer services are sustainable, are there markets for those services and how to provide them in an economically feasible way.

Consumption patterns in the Western countries and among affluent consumers elsewhere in the world have been pointed out as one of the ultimate sources of environmental degradation. Much of this unsustainable consumption occurs in the context of households, that is to say living at home and moving to and from it. A number of solutions, including service-based lifestyles, have been proposed to change the present consumption philosophies. The ways in which services are expected to make society more sustainable vary among the proponents of service thinking. Some of them see the 'service solution' from the information society perspective: as the structures of industrial production turn from manufacturing-dominated to information-intensive service models, de-linking of economic growth and environmental burden occurs (Bell, 1976; Jänicke et al, 1989). Some others take a 'less automatic' standpoint on the role of services. They do not foresee that an increasing share of services as a means of livelihood automatically reduces the environmental load. Instead they expect that in order to achieve eco-efficiency gains, service considerations must be crafted into models of production and consumption with the purposeful goal of reducing environmental impact of economic systems (Lovins, Lovins and Hawken, 1999). Within both streams of thinking, however, the sustainability of services has mainly been discussed from an eco-efficiency perspective rather than from a more holistic sustainability point of view. In other words, in the sustainable service literature, the social aspect of sustainability tends to be neglected at the cost of environmental and economic argumentation, which may be one of the reasons for the moderate success of eco-efficient services in the consumer market.

Moreover, citizen-consumers are often assumed to decide which products or services are being used. To some extent this is certainly true. However, depending on the consumption cluster (for example nutrition, mobility, or housing), households alone have only limited – greater or lesser, but still limited – possibilities to influence their patterns of consumption (Sanne, 2002; Roy, 2000). There are always other actors who are relevant in setting the frame for consumption choices. For instance with regard to housing and construction, property owners (housing providers), local authorities and service providers influence the housing framework. Or as regards mobility, local authorities and service providers have a lot to do with the transport infrastructure, and therefore they set the limits within which households are able to decide how to fulfil their mobility needs (Spangenberg and Lorek, 2002). This is another reason why it makes sense to seek for solutions for household sustainability with the service perspective in mind. Not only does this perspective capture the aspiration to shift consumption from products toward services, but it also takes into account other actors' possibilities to influence the households' consumption decisions.

To put it briefly, there are two major gaps in the sustainable service discussion: the lack of a holistic view of sustainability, and a disregard for the limited opportunity of households to influence their consumption choices. In order to include these issues, this book will put forth the idea of sustainable homeservices, propose some institutional arrangements with which to make them easily available for users, and explore the main drivers and hindrances for service-based household consumption.

The guiding questions of this book are:

- What are holistically sustainable household services and how to measure their sustainability?
- How to make consumers interested in using services that enhance sustainability?
- What kinds of delivery arrangements could enable the provision of such services?
- What kinds of business models suit the provision of sustainable household services and how to develop sustainable services?

This chapter starts with a brief discussion about services in general, and examines different types of eco-efficient services, as well as the ways in which they can reduce the use of material and energy resources. Following from the above-argued need to extend the eco-service discussion to explicitly include social or economic aspects, we will thereafter introduce the idea of a sustainable service – a concept that explicitly captures all sustainability dimensions. As we are interested particularly in consumer services that enhance sustainability, and argue that a considerable part of consumption relates to living at home, we introduce the concept, 'sustainable homeservices'. The underlying effort in this chapter is a progressively refined articulation of that concept. However, we start by first justifying why it makes sense to speak about sustainability, services, and homes in the same connection.

PRODUCTS, SERVICES OR SOMETHING IN BETWEEN?

How do services differ from products? Traditionally it is considered that services differ from products in four main respects. First, they are intangible, and secondly, in many service operations, production and consumption cannot be separated. Customers are involved and participate in the production process (for instance personal energy counselling to a household). To name a third difference, services are experienced differently by different customers (for instance, customers who cannot distinguish between physical goods, such as TV sets off the same production line, will normally be able to distinguish between services, for instance the different maintenance persons of the maintenance firm). Finally, services are perishable, in other words they cannot be stored (Baron and Harris, 2003; Zeithaml and Bitner, 1996; Payne 1993).

However, the difference between products and services becomes less pointed if we look at product and service offerings more closely. All products include some service, such as delivery, and all services require the use of some tangible elements, products (for instance premises) (Heiskanen and Jalas, 2003). This can be illustrated with Shostack's (1977) classical tangibility continuum (Figure 1). It is presented beneath with some examples adapted to the household service context. The model classifies products and services based on the amount of tangible and intangible elements (Baron and Harris 2003, Payne 1993).

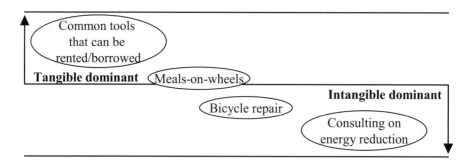

Figure 1. *Tangibility continuum adapted to the household services*

The definition of services suggested by Heiskanen and Jalas (2003) is the most suitable one for the present purpose, because it avoids the pitfall of service versus product definition. According to them, service is an added value for the customer, that is, an economic activity which replaces the customer's own labour with activities conducted by the service provider, either personally, automatically or in advance through planning and design.

SUSTAINABLE SERVICES ARE MORE THAN ECO-EFFICIENT

The discussion about 'sustainable services' or 'sustainable product-service systems' has tended to emphasise the eco-efficiency perspective rather than explicitly capture all sustainability aspects (Tukker, 2004; Roy, 2000). Particularly social or socio-economic considerations have received very little attention. This may be one of the underlying reasons why eco-efficient service concepts, especially those directed to consumers have not been as successful in the market as their proponents hoped. We argue that sustainability must be seen in a more comprehensive fashion in the service discussion and research, as a concept that includes ecological, social and economic aspect with an equal weight. The added value of eco-efficient services to consumers may actually often relate to considerations lying in the sphere of social sustainability (Hobson, 2002; McMakin, Malone and Lundgren, 2002).

However, in this section we will first discuss the ways that various services can contribute to eco-efficiency. As there is fairly abundant research on eco-efficient services, the following discussion outlines the main streams of research on the eco-efficiency of services and presents a typology of eco-efficient services. Thereafter we address the need to comprehend sustainable services as a more extensive concept than merely eco-efficient services and put forward the idea of adding the social dimension to sustainable service thinking.

Brief introduction to eco-efficient services

The notion of immateriality and intangibility often connected to services does not automatically lead us toward a more ecologically sustainable society (cf. Mont 2002; Heiskanen et al, 2001). There are, however, two main routes through which services can lead to a decreased environmental burden in society. The first one is the potential related to the general shift to services with a lower than average material intensity, such as medical or personal care, legal services, banking, and the like. From a macroeconomic perspective, the shift to services and thus the increased service intensity of the economy contributes to ecology through the decline of traditional smokestack and extractive industries in relation to less materials-intensive and more knowledge- and labour-intensive service industries. These services, however, are not necessarily eco-efficient. Their eco-efficiency must be assessed for each individual service and its context (cf. Salzman, 2000; Heiskanen et al, 2001).

As contended earlier, another route for approaching the ecological sustainability potential of services is the idea of eco-efficient services. According to that stream of research there are so-called eco-efficiency instances in which particular services or product-service combinations have the potential to reduce resource consumption while still fulfilling the same need of the consumer as the traditional alternative of owning the product. The ideas for eco-efficient service thinking come from many sources. One of its roots is in the so-called factor discussion that urges radical reductions in the intake of materials into the economy: by a factor of four (von Weizsäcker, Lovins and Lovins 1997) or by a factor of ten (Schmidt-Bleek 1998). This dematerialization and reduction in energy usage is expected to be achieved by fulfilling the needs of customers with the help of services instead of products, such as a car-sharing service instead of a private car. Services that replace products to a greater or lesser degree, and thus reduce the material and energy needed to perform an economic activity, for instance moving and cooking, are often called eco-efficient services. The above, however, is not to argue that all services replacing products are always necessarily more environmentally sound than a product fulfilling the same need. There are limitations to the eco-efficiency concept, such as the rebound effect (e.g. Jalas, 2002), but that as well as other critiques (e.g, Hukkinen, 2003) fall beyond the scope of this study.

It is possible to identify different types of eco-efficient services. They extend from conventional forms of renting, leasing and sharing to selling 'solutions' (e.g. integrated pest management) (Hockerts, 1999). A number of typologies have been developed in order to classify the broad range of services that can be seen to involve an eco-efficiency component. The classifications vary slightly depending on the author's line of reasoning. To draw an integrative classification based on the writings of Hockerts (1999), Heiskanen (2001), and Roy (2000), product-based services are services that are related to the use of a product. The product may be sold to the customer or not. In the former alternative the service component relates to repair, maintenance, upgrading or take-back of the product. The model can be seen as an example of extended responsibility of the producer even after the point of sale. The concept is relatively close to conventional manufacturing business – for instance the common practice of giving a guarantee extends the responsibility of the seller or producer of the product. Renting or leasing a product to the user goes a step further: the ownership remains with the producer. These kinds of services are sometimes also called use-oriented services, because only the use of product is being sold (e.g. in a car sharing concept, the use of the car is the offering). Use-oriented services can be divided into individual use and joint use. Leasing, renting and hire purchase are forms of individual use, whereas sharing and pooling are forms of joint use. These services produce potential environmental benefits because they lead to a more intensive use of fewer products by several consumers (Behrendt et al, 2003).

Result-oriented services are services within which the focus is on fulfilling customers' needs, and which are or seek to be independent of a specific product (therefore sometimes called need-oriented services). This type of services can be seen as including various forms of contracting, for instance least-cost planning in the energy sector, facility management, or waste minimization services. Result-oriented service may be offered by the manufacturer, such as an energy provider. It may be profitable for the provider to promote energy-saving equipment. A decrease in demand through gains in efficiency allows the energy company to increase its market share without having to build new power plants. However, these kinds of services are frequently provided by another company, for instance an energy service company (Hockerts, 1999; Heiskanen et al, 2001; Roy, 2000). Especially within the consumer market, they may be provided by another organization such as a public or non-profit organization, as will be exemplified later in this book. In the case of result-oriented services, the responsibility for supplying the goods required for the service lies with the service supplier. Initially, a craftsman's service such as the installation of a heating system can be classified as a result-oriented service. In the traffic sector, cab services, public transport and air traffic are included in the term. Transport services are generally defined by external factors and managed by professionals (such as taxi driver, pilot). Other examples include energy services, which aim to reduce energy consumption. Instead of selling units of electricity, what is sold are heat, light and cold. This way, the supplier is no longer tied to the production of one product. The producer's main task is to put the best system components together to satisfy customer's specifications and ecological aspects and to find the best overall system solution. Contracting, although not very common in households, can be considered a typical result-oriented service: the contractor is committed to the energy management of a property and the contract holder pays for these services (Behrendt et al, 2003).

Why would the services outlined above contribute to eco-efficiency – to be precise, to a reduction in materials and energy consumption? There are a number of reasons why efficiency benefits may accrue. Firstly, if the ownership of the product remains with the manufacturer, there is an incentive to produce more durable goods. This is because income is created by selling the use of the product, not the one-time sale of the product itself. Secondly, a smaller stock of products is needed if consumers use the same product in sequence. The smaller the stock of products, the less material is needed to produce them. In other words, more intensive use increases the probability of higher service yield before the product becomes obsolete due to outdated technological characteristics or fashion, for instance. Often, for example cars or personal computers are exchanged for newer ones not due to their breaking apart, but for reasons that lie somewhere in the midway between outdated technology and fashion. Thirdly, in result-based services in which the operator takes responsibility for product use, the service may facilitate more professional product use. To mention one more instance of the potential of services, the service model may contribute to the choice of a product that is more relevant to the task. For example, in a car-sharing system, the user may choose a car that fits the transportation task at hand: a small car for one person and a family car for multiple persons. This reduces instances of overkill: to be specific, choosing products that are too big or with too many accessories, just in order to be prepared for all possible contingencies (Heiskanen 2001), such as 'we need a bigger car because we sometimes take the grandparents with us'.

The social dimension of sustainable services

The observation that a large share of private consumption occurs in the context of households was one of the starting points for our interest in promoting the concept of sustainable homeservices. The eco-efficient service literature offers us some ideas to start with, but it is a new field of study and consequently there are still a number of 'blind spots' calling for attention. One of them is the above-mentioned absence of social aspects in sustainable service thinking (Gatersleben, 2001) and a limited understanding of economic considerations. The other one is inadequate attention to the question of how and by whom should sustainable services be provided in order to be used by consumers (Behrendt et al, 2003).

The present eco-efficiency discussion still typically uses the terminology of sustainability even though concentrating primarily on the eco-efficiency aspect of services (see for instance various writings available at the website of SusProNet 2004). When social and socio-economic impacts are acknowledged in eco-efficient service research, they tend to be mentioned in passing rather than being given equal weight as eco-efficiency (e.g. Mont, 2004; Vercalsteren and Gerken, 2004; Heiskanen and Jalas, 2003) Hence the concept of 'sustainable (home)service' is yet to be discovered and defined. We will try to take one of the first – rather pragmatic – steps here. The notion of sustainable development as defined by WCED (1987) offers one possible starting point for outlining the concept:

'In essence, sustainable development is a process of change in which the exploitation of resources, the direction of investments, the orientation of technological development, and institutional change are all in harmony and enhance both the current and future potential to meet human needs and aspirations.'

The notion stresses that all components – ecology, economy and societal considerations – should be in harmony for the development to qualify as sustainable. Consequently, for a service to be classified 'sustainable', it should have a positive impact on each of the areas of sustainability. However, a harmonious optimum is not always reachable. A service may have contradictory impacts vis-à-vis different dimensions of sustainable development, as we will see later in this book.

WHAT IS A SUSTAINABLE HOMESERVICE?

Services include those offered to organizational customers (i.e. business enterprises or other types of organizations) or to consumers. In this book we are interested in services offered to consumers, or to be precise to households consisting of one or more consumers. But we do not address all possible services offered to households. In the following we will elaborate what kind of services qualify for this study.

Very broadly speaking it could be said that homeservices are services offered to a consumer in connection to living at home. However, this definition is far too general and would easily encompass nearly all services that at least remotely relate to the consumer's daily life. In order for the ecological benefits to accrue, services with eco-efficiency potential should be offered to consumers at their home, or near to home (Behrendt et al, 2003). For instance, if the consumer uses a laundry instead of owning a washing machine, this may have positive effects in terms of less water and energy needed per load in large-scale operations, and in terms of a reduction in materials use due to the need for fewer washing machines (Goedkoop et al, 1999, Heiskanen et al, 2001). However, if the consumer has to drive three kilometres back and forth to do her laundry, gasoline use and exhausts released can outweigh the benefits gained. Furthermore, the findings of Behrendt et al. (2003) underscored the point that the consumers' willingness to use services with eco-efficiency potential decreases with the difficulty of reaching the service, such as distance or other conditions like difficulties in finding information (see also Peattie, 2001). Taking this standpoint it could broadly speaking be argued that:

Homeservices are services offered to consumers at home or on the housing premises – namely in their dwelling, in their building or on the building grounds.

Combined with the above reasoning about the concept of 'sustainable service', for the purpose of the present study homeservices are those household services that have a certain positive contribution to sustainable development in its environmental, social and economic dimension. The criteria for these dimensions will be elaborated in the next chapter. Consequently, we propose the general definition of sustainable home-services:

A sustainable homeservice is a service that is offered to the consumer on the housing premises and contributes positively to sustainable development in its environmental, social and economic dimensions.

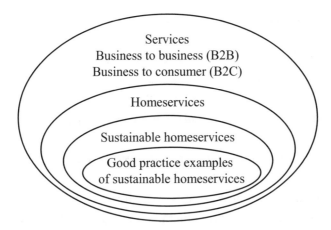

Figure 2. *Sustainable homeservices as a subset of services*

In our progressively defined articulation of the concept of a sustainable homeservices, we have now proceeded to the second-most inner circle of Figure 2. However, there is indication that a decision rule for judging a service sustainable only when it has a positive impact on all three areas of sustainability might be too strict (Hrauda et al, 2002). A service that causes a clear environmental improvement and increases comfort for the residents, but does not have a positive economic effect would be excluded from the definition of sustainable homeservices. The reality of today is that it is difficult to come across household services that would simultaneously fulfil all sustainability conditions – environmental, social and economic. For pragmatic reasons it may be useful in this early stage of sustainable household service development to accept that a sustainable service is one that satisfies two of the three sustainability criteria. However, it will depend upon the analyst what to accept as 'sustainable'. One of the risks in the policy of two dimensions is, for instance, that the environmental impact is neglected. At any event, the good-practice services presented and evaluated in this book are selected on the basis of the following pragmatic definition, although many of them contribute to all three dimensions.

Pragmatic definition of sustainable homeservice: a service that is offered to a consumer at home or on the premises, and contributes positively to sustainable development in at least two of its three dimensions.

CITIES, TOWNS AND SERVICE AREAS

Where can we start looking for sustainable homeservices? It is possible to identify a number of pressure points that connect sustainable development and households at different levels of analysis. For one, the rapid growth in the number of households taking place in many European countries imposes a major burden on infrastructure support (such as space, basic utilities provision, transport links), on the socio-economic system, and on the environment (Turner 1998). Moreover, responding to the trend of the ageing population in the European countries will either require building more and more old people's homes or providing a more sophisticated set of services in order to make it possible for the elderly to live at home by themselves. The former is often considered an economically unsustainable alternative, and is also less preferred by the elderly themselves.

Yet another pressure trend that can be highlighted in this connection is the household use of energy – for heating, domestic appliances and the car. Despite the fact that resource efficiency gains derived from technological improvements have accumulated – such as more efficient domestic heating systems, smaller or less energy consuming electrical appliances, and the installation of building insulation – these gains have been offset by the steep rise in the total number of households (which is due to the decreasing average size of households) (Turner, 1998). At the housing sector level, aggregate trends in resource use are continuing to rise. This implies that problems in the housing sector cannot be solved by technological solutions only but that social innovations are also needed. Sustainable service thinking is likely to offer one source of innovation. This is not to say that the evaluated services do not include any technological components. On the contrary, many of the good practice service examples identified are made possible by a technological element such as the use of advanced information and communication technologies (ICT).

Previous studies on sustainable households have focused on household functions or needs. These would involve e.g. shopping, cooking, eating, clothing care, shelter, personal hygiene, food storage and preparation, leisure activities within the home, and transportation (Vergragt, 2000; Gatersleben and Vlek, 1998). Within these functions, the researchers have tried to prepare scenarios of 'alternatives for more sustainable household' and study their feasibility (Vergragt, 2000). Even if household functions may be a good starting point for exploring new ideas for sustainable services, from the provider's perspective it might be worthwhile to approach the issue by looking at household service areas instead of functions. The following are some examples of housing and household service areas that can be relevant for housing organizations or other service providers vis-à-vis their service provision (see e.g. Scharp et al, 2000; Hrauda et al, 2002). The services evaluated for this book represent these seven areas:

1. Counselling & information (on environment and energy, social aspects, financial aspects)
2. Care & supervision (of buildings, dwellings, persons and pets)
3. Leisure activities (sports, social events, culture and communication, food services and catering)
4. Repairs (of furniture, appliances and the like)
5. Mobility & delivery (vehicle rental and sharing, delivery, other logistics)
6. Safety & security (of buildings, dwellings, persons)
7. Supply & disposal (energy and water supply, and waste disposal).

In order to understand how sustainable services fit into the overall service provision context in terms of the actors and the general service provision structure, we selected two locations in each country, where we investigated the household service supply in the above seven fields. Consequently, the analysed services are from one city and one smaller town in six countries: Austria (Vienna and Litschau), Finland (Helsinki and Kouvola), Germany (Berlin and Kleinmachnow), The Netherlands (Amsterdam and Heemstede), Portugal (Lisbon and Torres Vedras) and Spain (Bilbao and Zarautz). After scanning the general household service supply in these 12 locations, the good-practice sustainable service examples were chosen. Altogether over 200 examples were found. Their evaluation is presented in Chapter 2 and the housing and service situation in cities and towns is one of the topics of Chapter 3.

BLUEPRINT OF THE BOOK

This book is about services that are offered to consumers at their home and affect sustainable development positively in its ecological, social and economic dimensions. The starting point was that more eco-efficient lifestyles could be reached by substituting material- and energy-intensive consumption with services. Previous studies, however, indicate that in order for consumers to use services that at least partially replace resource-intensive consumption, these services must be available as conveniently as possible, preferably directly at home or on the premises. In essence, this book asks how to enhance sustainable development with more service-based consumption. The book consists of the following parts:

- Sustainable service examples and their evaluation with the Sustainability Evaluation Tool.
- The conditions for the demand for services. This comprises structural factors, which guide much of the behaviour of citizen-consumers, as well as consumer preferences with regard to service use.
- Investigation of the prominent providers, different forms of their cooperation and the delivery arrangements of services.
- Incentives and obstacles for sustainable household services in different countries.
- Business models of sustainable services and guidance for developing sustainable services.

Over 200 innovative service examples were selected on the basis of scanning the household service supply in altogether 12 locations, one city and one town in six European countries. We were keen on real-life service examples that are in operation in the market, not hypothetical concepts that sometimes drive the eco-efficiency research. The possibilities of the services to enhance sustainable development were assessed with a Sustainability Evaluation Tool that consists of 18 indicators of ecological, social and economic sustainability, and a related ordinal rating scale, with which the impact of the homeservice is compared to the situation where the service would not exist. The indicators seek to provide information on the following questions:

- Environment – What is the influence of homeservices on environment?
- Social – How do homeservices influence the well-being of consumers and the liveability of neighbourhoods?
- Economic – How do homeservices affect the economic situation of both the providers and users, as well as society at large?

The main strength of this method is that it is simple but yet it incorporates social and economic sustainability – which have tended to be bypassed in systematic analyses – with an equal weight as the ecological aspect. The analysis of the services sheds light on the missing links in creating competitive sustainable household services. One forgotten competitive element appears to be social sustainability in the service design. Good-practice examples of real-life services show that social sustainability, first and foremost the ability of services to improve the quality of life of their users – 'user pleasure' – is a crucial determinant for the competitiveness of services in the market place.

In order to further explore the opportunities for sustainable services, in addition to supply options the book addresses the demand for homeservices. Since demand is partially determined by a number of contextual and structural factors, an analysis of the housing situation and some socio-cultural items will be presented. In this connection the housing situation refers to items such as the income level with regard to housing expenditure, property structure, building structure and the city size. Nevertheless, consumer preferences also influence whether and which services are used. Consequently the book also includes the results of a personal interview survey of more than 300 consumers, and compares them with some previous findings. The findings imply that consumers appreciate the easy availability of services, such as getting multiple services via one contact. This means that there is room for service intermediaries providing access to several homeservices. As to consumers' willingness to pay, this seems to depend on the service. Consumers appear to be prepared to pay for coordinated repair services, care services and supply and disposal, whereas counselling and information services are mainly wanted for free.

The following part of the book deals with the providers of sustainable household services. Provided that services should be delivered to the homes of the customers or to the premises, for whom it would be economically feasible to offer them? In the eco-efficient service discussion it is typical to implicitly, if not explicitly, assume that business enterprises – often the large ones – are the main agents for sustainable household service provision. On the contrary, the present results indicate that large companies do not play a dominant role in provision of sustainable homeservices. Small and medium-sized enterprises, non-profit organizations and housing organizations are equally prominent. In addition, apart from their own services, public sector providers are often initiators or participants in supply arrangements involving multiple providers. In this context the previously omitted housing sectors actors, particularly housing organizations and housing management companies deserve special attention, since they bear close proximity to the consumers (residents), and are therefore in a position to offer or mediate the provision of services directly to the consumers' homes. It appears that innovative housing organizations already provide homeservices, either by themselves or in cooperation with other service providers. They are potential partners for providers or promoters of sustainable homeservices.

Chapter five deals with factors that can promote or hinder the supply of (sustainable) homeservices. Additionally some propositions for removing or circumventing the hindrances and, on the other hand, suggestions for utilizing the supportive trends are made. These factors stem from legislation and regulation, customer demand and market conditions, norms and practices of the housing or homeservice industry, or are caused by the infrastructure. Sometimes they are interrelated. Costs appear to be one of the main hindrances for service use in households. In some countries indirect labour costs add up the cost of homeservices considerably. In such instances, initiatives that reduce the tax burden of household service provision, or similar measures can be significant promoting factors for homeservice use. As to the customer demand or other market factors, the aging population and the increase in single households are Europe-wide phenomena that increase the potential demand for certain homeservices. This potential is, however, counteracted by lack of information on homeservices among the potential users and, secondly, the fact that those in need of services are often not used to using them, or cannot afford them. To reach these potential customers, different strategies are called for. These strategies as well as their compatibility with different national service use cultures are addressed.

The final part of the book asks what we can learn from both successful and incomplete elements of the business models of sustainable household services that are already in operation at the market. The business models of the good-practice sustainable homeservices are analysed with a framework concentrating on competitive advantage and customer benefits of the focal service, capabilities of the provider and the finance model of the service. The second of part of the chapter introduces a service engineering method that can be applied to the development of sustainable homeservices, both as concerns developing new services as well as improving the existing service offering of a provider.

In sum, the book illustrates how the homeservice approach can be used to promote sustainable consumption in a way that combines multiple benefits. In addition to reducing resource consumption, homeservices can increase the quality of life of their users and offer economically sound business opportunities for service providers, from private enterprises to non-profit and housing organizations. Combining these three pieces together however, requires background knowledge and information, which this book seeks to put forward.

2 Innovative homeservice examples and their sustainability effects

---

The concept of sustainable homeservices was defined in the first chapter. What did we find when searching for empirical examples of potentially sustainable services in the seven focal service areas? Before beginning the search for good examples, the concept of sustainable homeservice needed to be operationalized. For this purpose, we developed a relatively simple methodology for the assessment of the sustainability of services offered to households, called the Service Sustainability Evaluation Tool. The method is a fairly commonsensical approach, and its main contribution to the existing research is that it systematically develops indicators for not only environmental – which is the scope of much of the present indicator work – but also social and economic sustainability from the vantage point of household services. Furthermore, it seeks to integrate the different indicators into one screening instrument.

This chapter presents and illustrates the use of the Sustainability Evaluation Tool. But first we provide a brief overview of the number and types of homeservices that we found, as well as of the kinds of organizations providing them. After explaining the Sustainability Evaluation Tool, some of the good-practice services are described in detail in order to give a better idea of the variety of sustainable homeservices. The final section addresses the results of the evaluation, in other words the effects of household services on sustainable development.

Over 200 good-practice household services from 12 towns of six European countries were selected and evaluated with regard to their environmental, social and economic sustainability. In addition to the general investigation of sustainable service offerings, we paid particular attention to homeservices offered by housing organizations, because we wanted to examine 'services offered directly at the consumer's home or on the premises'. The eventual sample consists of sustainable homeservices provided by 19 housing organizations and 48 other providers (Table 1 and Table 2). Other providers include commercial enterprises, public providers and non-profit organiza- tions.

Table 1. *Number of service providers per country in the sample*

Number of service providers	Housing organizations	Other service providers	Sum
Austria	3	12	15
Germany	5	1	6
Netherlands	8	18	26
Spain	0	4	4
Finland	2	9	11
Portugal	1	4	5
Sum	19	48	67

As can be gathered from the figures, 67 providers for 215 services, some of the analysed providers offer more than one kind of service (Table 2). On the other hand, some services are co-produced by two or more providers. To give an example, some energy saving services are co-provided by a housing organization and another service provider, for instance an energy consultancy. It should also be noted that in some instances it was difficult to judge whether a service provider's offering is a single service or whether it actually contains a number of different services. For instance, there are providers that primarily label themselves as energy saving consultancies, but also provide advice on water conservation. In such cases we consider the offering as two separate services. Detailed descriptions of the analysed homeservices can be found at www.sustainable-homeservices.com.

Table 2. *Number of homeservices analysed by type of provider*

Services offered by different providers	By housing organizations	By other service providers	Co-produced services	Sum
Austria	17	56	1	74
Germany	19	4	3	26
The Netherlands	3	34	22	59
Spain	0	10	0	10
Finland	7	31	1	39
Portugal	1	5	1	7
Sum	47	140	28	215

We should emphasize that the sample of homeservices is a varied set of services. The analysed services do not include all possible sustainable homeservices in the respective 12 towns. Therefore the figures in Table 1 and Table 2 do not imply that this is the total amount of relevant services in all locations, let alone throughout all the countries. However, the selected homeservices are based on an extensive search, and they are representative for the assessment of the sustainability effects discussed in the next section.

In terms of the type of service providers and the number of services analysed, the sample varies from one country to another. The main reason for this variation is that the housing situation and the related services depend on the institutional and cultural context of housing in each country. One reason for the smaller number of homeservices in the Portuguese and Spanish samples was that good-practice sustainable homeservices do not yet exist in abundance in these countries. Furthermore, there are hardly any large (social) housing organizations in Portugal and Spain, and the existing few only cater for the lowest income class. Services are not within their scope of action. In Spain and Portugal the main form of housing is the condominium association. These are only legal entities that do not seem to offer homeservices contributing to sustainability. In the German sample, however, the relatively small number of analysed service providers is due to the fact that multiple services of five large housing organizations, instead of single services of multiple providers, were included in the analysis. We decided that the German team should concentrate particularly on the role and possibilities of housing organizations as homeservice providers, because rental housing has a large share in the German housing market and many housing organizations are engaged in homeservice provision as initiating or cooperating institution. Only one other type of service provider, an environmental organization offering multiple homeservices, Die Grüne Liga, was chosen for analysis from Germany although there would have been other prominent service providers, as well.

THE SUSTAINABILITY EVALUATION TOOL

A typical approach for evaluating the level of sustainable development in different contexts is to draft sustainability indicators. Such indicators have been drafted by different constituencies, for instance the Commission on Sustainable Development (CSD) (UNDSD, 2002), the Human Development Index (HDI) by UNDP (UNDP, 2001), Sustainable Consumption Indicators by UNEP (Bentley and de Leeuw, 2003), OECD (OECD, 1999, OECD, 2001) and the Daly-Cobb Index of Sustainable Economic Welfare (ISEW) (Mannis, 1998). However, so far no coherent indicators have been developed either for household consumption or for the related services (Lorek, 2002). None of the above indicators is suitable as such. Namely, they are mainly suited for national level analyses. Another concern from the perspective of this study is that many of them are at such a basic needs level that they do not make much sense in developed country contexts, but are better suited for assessing the urgencies of less developed countries. For example, the CSD indicator for housing is 'floor area per person'. A CSD-indicator for urbanization of the population is 'population of urban formal and informal settlements'. Nevertheless, these indicators can serve as one source for pointing out areas within which sustainability indicators for micro-level services related to household or housing could be developed. Furthermore, some of them offer an aggregate indicator from which to work downwards to develop more micro-level determinants for assessing whether the focal service has a positive sustainability effect.

Developing micro-level indicators for environmental sustainability is slightly easier than for social and economic ones, since some work has already been done both on indicators for the environmental impacts of household consumption (Lorek and Spangenberg, 2001; cf. also Bentley and de Leeuw, 2003) and on assessing the eco-efficiency potential of services (Heiskanen, 2001; Hockerts, 1999). Hockerts (1999) proposes a test of the eco-efficiency of a service according the following indicators: longer-life option, lesser material and energy consumption during use, revalorisation potential and efficiency of use. Heiskanen and Jalas (2003), on the other hand, adopt a more general perspective and suggest that benefits resulting from the shift from products to services can be: lower manufacturing volume, less impact during the use phase of the product, lower stock of products, and higher rate and quality of utilization of end-of-life products. The environmental indicators of household consumption developed by Spangenberg and Lorek (2002) and Lorek and Spangenberg (2001), include some that can be *drawn upon* – not used as such – for developing criteria for assessing the environmental potential of services directed to households. These include indicators for heating energy consumption, resource intensity, living space, organic products, food transportation, shopping and recreation transport distances, modes of transport for commuting, shopping and recreation purposes, and number of passenger cars.

The social and economic indicators perhaps warrant more discussion here because they have not been previously studied to the same extent as the environmental ones, neither at the household nor at the macro level (Lehtonen, 2004). Compared to the environmental aspect, there is a lack of tools to assess social sustainability (Lehtonen, 2004; Vercalsteren and Gerken, 2004). The proposed social and economic indicators have mainly been developed on the basis of the macro-level indicators discussed above and the quality-of-life indicators suggested by Gatersleben (2001) as well as the findings of housing studies by Scharp et al. (2000) and Hohm et al. (2002). From the latter ones we can draw upon comfort, health, safety, freedom/control, social justice, social relations, and education and development. Two indicators, work and income, which are considered social indicators by Gatersleben (2001), are treated here as indicators for economic sustainability. Some of these indicators, such as health, education, safety and security together with employment can also be found in the writings of Sen (1999) as components of 'freedom', which according to Sen should be the measure of development, instead of for instance GNP growth or related measures.

Our proposal for a set of indicators for assessing the ecological, social and economic sustainability of a homeservice is presented in Table 3. These indicators are meant for a simple assessment of a service, not for a comprehensive life-cycle analysis or for calculating the ecological footprint of a household. We find that for the first steps of starting to integrate all sustainability elements into service evaluation, a simple assessment device is sufficient. Furthermore, we wanted to propose a set of indicators and criteria that are feasible also for practitioners. Using the above-mentioned indicator studies as the background, we ended up with 18 indicators: six for environmental aspects, seven for social items, and five for economic sustainability. It should be emphasised that the suggested contents for the indicators are not exclusive, but should rather be treated as indicative of what issues to consider when assessing the service according to the particular indicator. The indicators in Table 3 are most probably easiest to understand when considered in combination with the method suggested for their operationalisation in Table 4.

Table 3. *A set of indicators for sustainable homeservices*

Environmental aspects	Social Aspects	Economic Aspects
1 Material use	7 Equity	14 Employment
2 Energy use	8 Health	15 Financial situation of the residents
3 Water use	9 Safety and security	16 Regional product and service use
4 Waste	10 Comfort	17 Profitability for the provider
5 Space use	11 Social contacts	18 Profitability for the region / community
6 Emissions	12 Empowerment	
	13 Information and awareness	

To elaborate on the social sustainability indicators in some more detail, 'equity' refers to the questions whether the service improves equality between people, whether it helps to combat social exclusion, and whether it promotes fair trade. The 'health' indicator evaluates whether the service contributes to preventing mental or physical illness. The 'safety and security' indicator relates to crime and vandalism prevention in the neighbourhood, and/or to the potential of the service to reduce risk of injuries. 'Comfort' refers to the effect of the service on reducing annoyance such as noise, odour, and/or pollution, on helping residents to save time, or on increasing convenience for the residents. Under the indicator 'social contacts', we would look at whether the service promotes social self-help like barter shops and swap internet sites, promotes communication in the neighbourhood or improves the neighbourhood atmosphere in general. 'Empowerment', on the other hand, refers to opportunities to exercise one's own volition and interact with and influence the world in which one lives (cf. Sen 1999). In a homeservice context, this refers to issues like improved opportunities for participation, or the provision of new channels for residents toward decision-makers (e.g. electronic ones). Some may find that there is overlap between equity and empowerment, but in terms of evaluation, we considered that equity refers to making individuals in disadvantaged positions more equal with those that do not suffer such disadvantages. Empowerment, on the other refers to instances of improved opportunities of participation of any individual. In specific instances an interconnection between these indicators can be that empowering individuals increases their equity. Thus empower-ment could be a source of equity, albeit a partial one. Lastly, under 'information and awareness' we would assess whether the service increases training, awareness and skills of the residents (Halme et al, 2004a).

As to the economic set of indicators, the most self-evident item on the list is perhaps 'employment'. It refers to whether the service creates new jobs, helps to secure existing ones, or helps to tackle long-term unemployment. In this connection one should consider what kind of employment is in question, for instance full-time permanent vs. temporary or part-time work. The 'financial situation of the residents' indicator comprises issues like residents' ability to save money or create more income as a result of the service. The following indicator 'regional products and service use' seeks to record whether the service increases the use of regional products or services. The indicator 'profitability for the provider' attempts to answer questions like: is the service profitable in the long-term (for its provider, such as the housing organization, or some other service provider); and/or does the economic efficiency of the whole service system improve? It does not only refer to the profitability of a business enterprise. Finally, the indicator 'profitability for the region/community' seeks to assess the effect of the service on the regional economy in a more general sense than the preceding indicator, 'regional product and service use'.

As to assessing the sustainability of homeservices, there is a particular problem. It stems from the fact that we are looking at open systems. It is not only difficult, but in many cases impossible, to draw a meaningful boundary around the 'system where the service has its influence'. In an open system, the problem arises that we do not have a fixed point against which the potential impact of the service should be measured. Even in a simple case, if we look at a particular building and a service offered to its residents, it may be possible to see, for instance that a common room reduces the need for individual space, but it cannot be measured exactly how much space is being saved – the result would always remain to some extent hypothetical (Halme et al, 2004a).

The task is further complicated by the fact that the analysed services also have other than direct effects. Occasionally the indirect effects of a service can be considerable. Consequently it would not be justified to omit them. Let us take an example of the effects of an organic food delivery service. The direct effects result from reductions in vehicle emissions, since one trip can be made from the farmer to the consumers, instead of several by the individual consumers to the farmer. As to the indirect effects, the service promotes organic farming and food, and the indirect effects are, for instance environmentally less harmful soil treatment and healthy nutrition. We have scored these kinds of indirect effects in the service evaluation presented later in the chapter.

Subsequently, our criteria for assessing the sustainability of homeservices are bound to be 'relative' or qualitative criteria, indicating a move in a positive direction, for instance 'increasing employment' or 'promoting environmentally friendly transport' – or in a negative, unsustainable direction. No absolute value is involved. The next question to ask is what amount of improvement counts for a criterion to be fulfilled? This is occasionally problematic, especially with regard to some social and economic criteria. How to judge if a service increases equity? Or whether it promotes the regional economy (almost any service gives some kind of an input to the regional economy)? Here we are, in the worst case, left with only the gut feeling of a mixed group of experts as a basis for assessment (Halme et al, 2004a).

How to assess a service on the basis of the above indicators, that is, how to operationalise them? Due to the above concerns, we propose a five-point ordinal scale for each indicator. The homeservices identified as potentially sustainable can be rated along this scale. Table 4 depicts the rating scale with one indicator as an example from each sustainability dimension. As mentioned above, the proposed indicators are relative, which means that they indicate a move in a positive (or negative) direction, for instance a reduction in waste or an increase in employment. For a relative method, the point of reference is an important element. For our method, the point of reference is the 'status quo' alternative in which the service does not exist (i.e. the 'current situation' or the 'do nothing/base line scenario'). If no change results from introducing the service, this would score 0 on the scale. Together Table 3 and Table 4 form the Sustainability Evaluation Tool applied later in this chapter for the assessment of the sustainability effects of selected homeservices.

Table 4. *Operationalization of sustainability indicators (example of one indicator in each sustainability dimension)*

Material use (environmental): The effect of the service on material use compared to status quo (status quo = situation without the service)
$\qquad$ -2 -1 0 1 2
Increases material use $\qquad$ Decreases material use
Empowerment (social): The effect of the service on residents' ability to influence decision-making that affects them
$\qquad$ -2 -1 0 1 2
Decreases the ability to $\qquad$ Increases the ability to influence influence
Employment (economic): The effect of the service on the employment
$\qquad$ -2 -1 0 1 2
Less jobs/job opportunities lost $\qquad$ More jobs are created

Explanation. 2 = a major positive change; 1 = a substantial positive change; 0 = the service does not make a change to status quo; -1 = a substantial negative change; -2 = a major negative change

When applied in service development or assessment, the results of these indicators are not always unambiguous. If they are applied in practice for homeservice development, it is important to pay attention to the functional linkages between the indicators. Improving a service with regard to one dimension may lead to adverse effects in another (Gatersleben, 2001). For instance, a swimming pool in the building may increase the comfort and health of residents, but it is likely to increase energy and water use, for instance, compared to a common swimming pool which can be used by a larger number of people. Furthermore, when assessing the sustainability effects of a service, it is important to note that they may occur at different levels. Most often they are at the micro-level (household, apartment building) but they can also take place on a more macro-level (neighbourhood, region, country). The key point is, however, to pay attention to the fact that despite the potential positive micro-level effects, there may be negative impacts in the larger system, and vice versa (Dovers, 1995; cf. also Wolf and Allen, 1995).

Some good-practice innovative sustainable homeservices will be illustrated in the next section. As mentioned in Chapter 1, in practice it is still today difficult to find homeservices that clearly contribute to all dimensions of sustainability. Consequently, for the purposes of this book, the decision rule was applied that if a service fulfils *at least two of the three sustainability conditions,* it will qualify for the sample of sustainable homeservices. For instance, a service that causes a clear environmental improvement and increases comfort for the residents, but does not have a positive economic effect can be included in the list of sustainable homeservices.

INNOVATIVE SERVICE EXAMPLES

The homeservice examples found in operation in the six European countries from North to South are best described as social innovations. Some of them make use of technological components such as ICTs, but the social features tend to be the crucial part of the services evaluated for this book. In essence it appears that sustainable homeservices placed on the market so far are mundane services that in one way or another support the everyday lives of their user-consumers. It turned out that some of the most appealing service concepts formed clusters, which in one sense can be a more interesting way of looking at these services than the originally applied seven service areas. The clusters according to which the innovative sustainable service examples below are organized consist of:

- Energy services;
- Repair and recycling services;
- Home delivery services of ecological groceries;
- Several homeservices from the same counter;
- Wide-range environmental counselling; and
- Ordinary services with eco-features.

Energy services

We found multiple homeservices aimed at reducing energy consumption, especially in the Netherlands, Finland and Germany. Some of these services were mainly based on counselling concepts. They primarily aimed to inform residents about less energy consuming behaviour patterns and to guide them toward these. But the services also involved measuring and screening elements and cost savings calculations. Other concepts were energy contracting by housing organizations aiming at energy savings, and installing energy saving equipment in the apartments or the building. Next, some counselling and contracting based examples are introduced.

Energy Expert service of Motiva Ltd. (Centre for Energy Efficiency), Finland

Energy experts are residents who have been trained to be active in energy issues in the building they live. Energy experts monitor sudden changes in the energy/electricity/heating consumption on the basis of energy and water consumption data provided by the housing organization or the energy company. They give advice to other residents on energy efficiency and conservation issues. They also act as the residents' contact person toward the housing organization and housing management company and vice versa.

The Centre for Energy Efficiency (Motiva) co-ordinates both the energy expert training and further development of the concept. Motiva is a limited company but it operates under the Ministry of Trade and Industry and receives part of its funding from it. Motiva also maintains extranet pages for experts and for trainers, and it keeps a list of the qualified trainers' network. Trainers do the actual teaching and training. Motiva developed the expert concept together with the social housing organization VVO, which was the first organization to apply the concept in 1994. Today VVO has about 500 energy experts among its tenants. Since 1994, Motiva has trained altogether 3000 energy experts in Finland.

This service contributes positively to all sustainability dimensions. As to environmental and economic benefits, an active energy expert can have a substantial effect on the energy and water consumption and consequently the operating costs. In the buildings with active energy experts, the average reductions in resource use are five per cent in heating, ten per cent in electricity consumption and 20 per cent in water usage. Lower costs reduce a housing organization's or condominium association's pressure to increase rents or utility charges.

According to VVO and some residents of houses with energy experts, the social benefits are also evident. The energy expert concept increases especially the skills and awareness of the residents who become experts. These skills and knowledge spread when experts disseminate information about the effects of energy consumption or other resource use in a constructive way and give positive examples of how energy and water efficiency can save resources and offer economic benefits for the residents/tenants. Energy experts have also been found to contribute positively to social contacts among the residents and to give residents a smooth communication channel toward the housing management.

Advisory Board on Utility Costs, housing organization WBG Marzahn, Germany

A somewhat similar concept that makes use of residents' voluntary contributions can be found in Berlin. In 2000, the Berlin housing company WBG started a campaign to motivate its residents to save utility costs by reducing their resource and energy consumption. After having modernised most of its 32,000 dwellings according to new energy-saving standards, the WBG Marzahn began to inform its residents broadly on potentials to save resource related costs in order to make the renovation measures effective. Apart from training 50 employees into so-called 'utility cost skilled consultants', the housing company established an 'advisory board on utility costs' composed of engaged tenants who analyse utility cost developments and inform other tenants on saving potentials. Thus, the WBG Marzahn is faced with critical control of its management practices, but profits equally from improved trust on the part of its tenants.

Considerable savings of utility costs and resource consumption in the WBG's dwellings proved that the 'advisory board on utility costs' reached its goal successfully. The tenants' engagement in supporting the service contributes to strengthened neighbourly relationships and a community feeling. By disclosing the company's utility cost management, WBG promotes tenants' participation in decisions, thus supporting the residents' empowerment. Residents as well as the housing organization profit from reduced housing costs. As the Advisory Board on Utility Costs consists of volunteering tenants, it does not entail considerable financial investments.

EPA tailor-made energy reduction advice, The Netherlands

The Dutch energy advice concept is based fully on professional experts' work rather than involving voluntary residents in the service delivery. EPA (Energy Performance Advice) is a national governmental subsidy program. Owners of dwellings built before 1998 can apply for an EPA by approaching an EPA adviser. The adviser will pay a short visit to the dwelling and report back about which energy-saving measures are possible (for example, additional insulation or double-glazing) and cost-efficient. The service is subsidized and provides advice on the costs, energy savings, subsidies and return on investment related to the proposed measures.

As to the sustainability effects, the service is focused on the reduction of energy. But on the other hand it has a potential negative environmental effect due to the increase in materials use (for example insulation materials). From a social point of view, the service has a positive effect on the resident's comfort, information and awareness. In addition to energy facts and improvement possibilities regarding their dwelling, residents can benefit from additional features, such as double glazed windows that decrease the annoyance from noise. Moreover the service saves the residents' time since the provider pays a visit at home. From an economic point of view, the implementation of the advice can be a big investment for the residents, but on the other hand the owners of the dwelling are typically already on the verge of remodelling their home, and they receive extra subsidy. In the long term they usually save on energy costs.

Energy contracting of housing organizations

The partnership between the Berlin housing cooperative Bremer Höhe and the Berlin Energy Agency is a good practice of energy contracting. The service aims at reducing housing costs and emissions by integrated concepts for efficient energy use. Providing a full service from counselling to the installation of heating facilities and constant cost management, energy contracting agencies offer efficient lifecycle management to the housing organization, which results in sustained cost savings for both the resident and the housing organization.

In general, energy contracting consists of an evaluation of the existing heating facilities and possible saving potentials by new contracts or techniques. Hereupon, the energy contractor mediates between energy suppliers, producers of technical equipment and the housing organization to negotiate good conditions for his customer. Finally, the contractor manages all necessary construction measures and arranges legal frameworks to minimize current cost. In most cases the pay-back period of investments is short. Moreover, residents get counselling on construction measures and energy saving, as they have to commit themselves to use exclusively the new equipment for heating or electricity.

Energy contracting is one of the most successful instruments to combine ecological and economic benefits in the housing sector. The combined heat and power units at the Bremer Höhe reduce CO_2 emissions by over 40 per cent (450 t/a). Energy contracting combined with individual energy counselling promotes the residents' awareness of environmental issues and of their contribution to resource conservation. Residents at the Bremer Höhe pay about 0.67 €/m² a month for heating and warm water, which is less than the Berlin average. So both residents and landlord benefit from energy contracting.

The Finnish nation-wide housing organization VVO contracts for green electricity. Eco-labelled electricity costs slightly more than ordinary electricity, which tends to put off many potential customers. However, since VVO procures electricity in bulk, it gets discounts. Due to the discounts the price per kWh comes down to the price level of ordinary electricity. Thus VVO can buy green electricity for its apartment buildings and still charge only the normal price from its residents.

Repair and recycling services

Interesting repair services were hard to find, but there were a few highly relevant examples. In addition to the evident environmental sustainability benefits of recycling and repair service concepts, such homeservices appear to contribute to social sustainability. We introduce four services to exemplify the concepts in this cluster.

R.U.S.Z. and T&T – recycling and repairing in Vienna and Helsinki

R.U.S.Z. is a non-profit organization that repairs or dismantles a wide range of household appliances. These appliances are gathered from waste collection sites or are picked up from or delivered by individual households. Usable parts from irreparable appliances are salvaged for repairing other appliances. Furthermore, hazardous substances are removed and disposed of appropriately. R.U.S.Z. repairs competitively and gives a one-year warranty on the appliances. Individual households can also rent or buy household appliances that R.U.S.Z. has fixed at competitive prices. R.U.S.Z. also offers other organizations the maintenance of their equipment and appliances. It also works together with Viennese evening schools, offering repair courses.

A fairly similar service of T&T, a Finnish social enterprise, consists of collecting discarded electronic household and office equipment and repairing it for sale or recycling it for industrial use. The collection is done by both pick-ups and reception at their facilities. Repaired appliances are sold in T&T's 'recycling shop' for households. Dismantled materials are sold to industries for reprocessing. T&T also recycle batteries, furniture, etc. T&T is also planning to work together with a local government housing company – Maunula Apartments – and a local non-governmental organization called Maunula-Apu (Maunula-Help). Together they have a pilot project for collecting electronic appliances and scrap metal within the building premises.

Vis-à-vis sustainability effects, these services prolong the life cycle of the electronic appliances and substantially reduce the amount of electronic household and office appliances waste. As they are not linked to the manufacturer or seller of any household appliance, their main interest is really to repair instead of recommending that the customer buy a new appliance. Social benefits accrue because these enterprises employ long-term unemployed, immigrant, disadvantaged and disabled people. They also enhance the working skills of their employees with the aim of enabling them to employ themselves on the open labour market. About 60 per cent of T&T's employees have obtained jobs in the commercial sector. Another important social aspect is the offer of repaired appliances at a low price catering to low-income individuals and families.

Economically this service concept is beneficial because it creates new job opportunities for people who have been unemployed or might have other difficulties in getting jobs in the commercial sector. At the moment of writing this, T&T is partially economically self-sufficient and partially funded by the EU and the City of Helsinki. R.U.S.Z. is financed by the City of Vienna and the investment of the city is planned to pay off in three years. However, when the WEEE (Directive on waste of electronic and electrical equipment) directive becomes fully enforced, it is expected to be economically self-sufficient. However, the future of recycling electronic and electrical appliances as well as other energy using products is relatively unpredictable at the moment, because large industrial recycling networks are also being established in different European countries in order to enforce the requirements of the WEEE and EuP (energy using products) directives.

Emaus – Collection, repair and sale of used products, Spain

The Emmaus Foundation is an international non-profit organization, with the mission of combining the collection, repair and sale of used products with initiatives for socially handicapped groups. Its mission is to fight against extreme poverty, and it operates in 38 countries in five continents (Emmaus International 2005). One of the member associations is the Emaus Group in Gipuzkoa, which started its activity in the 1980s. After a redefinition of its operations in 1992, the productive activities of Emaus were organized in the form of different workers' cooperatives. The productive activities, which started out with 15 employees in 1994, now employ about 37 people in Gipuzkoa, more than half of them long-term unemployed, who have passed some kind of support program for reintegration into working life.

Emaus runs a fleet of its own trucks, which collect furniture, textiles, electrical appliances, books and other products from households. Emaus then separates the products for repair and sale, or recycling or disposal. Repaired products are sold in Emaus' own stores, either at the foundation's premises or in one of the four outlets in San Sebastian.

In addition to the social effect of employing people from disadvantaged groups, there are environmental sustainability effects. Seventy-four per cent of the household waste collected by Emaus can be reused directly, another 24 per cent can be recycled and only two per cent goes into final disposal or treatment. Emaus offers commercial routes for many smaller second-hand products, which would otherwise end up among the general household waste.

Emaus now has a sound economic basis, although its long-term development depends on pending legislation on recycling. The productive activities (waste collection and re-sale) generate an income of approximately €759,000 (year 2002). During last year, no subsidies were received, which shows some independence from the public administration. Additionally, approximately €230,000 of tax payments were generated. The service reduces the cost of collecting waste in the municipalities by 50 per cent and adds up savings from lower disposal and treatment costs for the landfilling of textiles, furniture and electric and electronic appliances as well as from reduction in public aid (employment benefits and social allowances).

Bàh – Bicycle repair at home, The Netherlands

Báh, bicycle repair at home is a small-scale service, but we present the example here since in the consumer interviews it appears that this is one of the services that people would be very willing to use. Bàh is a one-man enterprise providing bicycle repair service at the customer's premises in the city of Utrecht. Clients can contact Bàh by phone, by filling in an application form on the website or by sending an email. Bàh can come in the evening or on the weekend to a customer's home to repair the bike. The entrepreneur gives a three-month guarantee on mended tubes. The price for repairs is set in advance.

The reason that this service is so popular is that it is cumbersome to transport a broken bicycle to the repair store unless one has a car – and moreover a sufficiently large one. An indirect environmental sustainability effect that can be hypothesized is that this kind of service helps people not to stop cycling for a while because of the difficulty and reluctance of finding bike transport to a mending facility (and thus switch over to using a car, for instance). A less hypothetical positive effect on the environment is the fact that the provider does not need space for a workshop. This also means a reduced investment and overhead costs for Bàh. The service provides comfort to the residents as they do not have to go with their broken bike to a repair shop. While mending the bicycle, the mechanic likes to teach his customers, thereby offering a learning experience for those interested.

Home delivery of ecological food and groceries

There are a number of delivery services that offer organic (and often local) food and ecological groceries. They are interesting due to a number of sustainability benefits that are involved. Organic food is produced without the use pesticides and many considered it to have a positive effect on health. Ecological grocery shops tend to make more use of regional products than ordinary shops. This stimulates the regional economy. However, the delivery of groceries is more expensive than shopping in an ordinary grocery store.

The business ideas of ecological food delivery services vary. On one hand there are small-scale operations like family-owned Txillarre in the Basque country, Spain, delivering organic farming products via internet orders. On the other hand there are service providers like Biowichtl, a commercial provider in Austria that offers and delivers a wide range of organic foods directly from organic farmers or from co-operatives, as well as cosmetics. These kinds of services are often necessary for getting organic food to customers in the first place, because the normal supermarket channel is not a feasible option. However, delivery by car is the questionable part of such services, and when compared to the normal supermarket logistics, a lot depends on how the delivery routes and the surrounding conditions are organized.

Eko-Direkt is an Amsterdam-based company that started delivering ecological groceries to home by bicycle. It is formed by three environmentally oriented enterprises (Eko-direct, CW-the Belly4 and Versnelling). The service combines an internet grocery shop with environmentally friendly products and two delivery bicycle enterprises. Ecological groceries are ordered via the internet. On the website an extensive selection of eco-friendly groceries such as drinks, body care products and cleaning detergents are available. Users can compile personalized shopping lists for further use. By clicking on the items it is possible to get extra information about the product, like the type of eco-label it carries. The website also has links with additional information which increases the customers' awareness about healthy food. Delivery is done by bicycle, reducing the need to use the car for home transport. Payment is done by weekly authorisation. As Eko-Direkt's business as well as the delivered amounts grew, the company began to also deliver by a small electric car and a larger ordinary car. The firm still seeks to keep the transportation as environmentally sound as possible.

Several homeservices from the same counter

One of the main obstacles for consumers to use services in their everyday lives is that they are too difficult to find. There are some organizations that seek to advance household service use by simplifying the process of finding homeservice providers. They also seek to address the reliability issue, because another threshold for increased homeservice use is the question of the trustworthiness of the service provider.

The Finnish Work Efficiency Institute has set up an internet market place for providers and customers of homeservices, ELIAS. The service is free for people who are looking for services and for the companies that advertise their services in ELIAS. Services offered include cleaning, gardening, small repairs, food services, health care services, errand services, walking assistance and other services. At the moment ELIAS lists providers from Southern Finland, offering contact information for more than 400 service providers. The service as such is simple, but it has features that make it very popular among customers. Firstly, the Work Efficiency Institute screens the providers to make sure that they are registered companies. Secondly, it encourages feedback from service users and if it appears that the service provider is not reliable, the provider is removed from the list. Secondly, ELIAS gives a quality rating to its services. Employees of a company that wishes to market its services on this internet site have to go through a basic training concerning service quality before they can be listed on the internet service. The training also includes eco-efficiency aspects of service production. After the compulsory training it is possible to take a voluntary 'two star-training' on service quality and provision. The third, three-star certification can be obtained if the service provider has vocational qualifications or a degree from a certified school.

The site also offers advice to homeservice users on tax deduction possibilities of service costs and on other fiscal matters related to the use of home services. In addition a standard contract form that can be applied between buyer and service provider is provided on the website. During the first years the service is partially funded by EU and the regional government, which wants to promote employment in the service industry. The results have exceeded expectations. ELIAS has eased customers' access to homeservices and created new business for small service providers who have fewer possibilities to market their services. Thus it has helped to secure existing jobs and to create new ones.

A somewhat similar service concept from Spain, Buenos Dias/Buenas Noches (BDBN), is a membership-based non-profit organization operating in the greater Bilbao area. It mediates homeservices from several providers. Individuals wishing to use BDBN pay an annual fee of 100 € for membership. By calling BDBN, they get the service provider to their home. For a number of services like a doctors' visit or plumbing, there is a guarantee that the service is delivered at a certain time. If not, the BDBN compensates the price. Customers get discounts for the market price of the services.

To give one more example of 'multiple services from the same counter', some Austrian housing organizations are setting up service centres, which in addition to normal maintenance services offer extra services like cleaning, laundry services or child sitting. They do not provide all of them with their own personnel but network with other service providers. The service centres also recommend and give contact information for many other homeservices.

Wide-range environmental counselling service

Some of the good practice services can be termed wide-range environmental counselling services. For one, the German Green League (Die Grüne Liga) is a network of 29 member groups that offer social and ecological services. It has three main fields of action. One is a counselling service on organic nutrition. The network also mediates home delivery of organic vegetables. Secondly the Green League does counselling for civic initiatives in the field of Local Agenda 21, nature conservation and protection of species. Accordingly, they help people to protect and restore their natural environment, for instance by giving legal advice to initiatives that aim at preserving a biotope in their neighbourhood. Furthermore, they inform citizens on participation processes. The third service area is sustainable development of neighbourhoods, which translates as giving advice on subjects such as ecological construction and renovation, rain water management, greening of backyards or domestic pollutants. Based on a situation analysis, the Green League develops concepts and gives advice on legal matters as well as possible subsidies. Another important activity of the Green League is to protect urban biotopes as well as endangered urban species such as special birds or bats.

The Green League's counselling on ecological housing has a positive effect on resource consumption through activities such as reduced material use or promoting the use of rainwater. In addition, concentrating on local service providers and producers reduces emissions due to transport of goods. The Green League strengthens small networks of local service providers in the field of organic agriculture and counselling on ecological housing or civic initiatives.

In Austria, Umweltberatung (Environmental counselling) is a decentralised non-profit organization that offers consulting on all environmental issues of households, supports other educators with projects and research and disseminates information in numerous publications and online. A large part of the work is done in cooperation with the national and district agencies. There are 14 information centres in Austria, offering primarily telephone counselling in the whole country. Counselling for individuals is free of charge, unlike some of the consulting for business enterprises. Income from business customers helps the organization to cover some of their costs, and provide free advice to private households.

Environmental benefits are related to the dissemination of environmental knowledge within the population, with a change of attitude and behaviour regarding waste prevention, organic gardening, healthy nutrition, ecological building materials, energy efficiency and biodegradable cleaning products.

Ordinary services with eco-features

We found a number of service examples where the service concept as such is quite ordinary, but becomes more relevant when an ecological feature is added to it. Some of these examples are briefly highlighted here. Eco-Care is a Dutch gardening service company developing natural gardens that need limited maintenance efforts. The employees use neither pesticides nor artificial fertilizers. Furthermore, when constructing a garden they try to re-use materials where possible. Eco-Care follows the newest developments in ecological gardening and works with a personal approach. After an intensive personal interview, Eco-care makes a creative design for the garden that fits the customer's personality. For customers who prefer to do the gardening themselves, Eco-care offers courses on ecological gardening.

A Spanish architecture and construction company Abil is specialized in ecological construction and renovation projects, characterized by the use of ecological materials, reduction of energy consumption and the reuse of materials whenever possible. The company uses mostly natural materials such as timber, inert materials for bricklaying (plaster of Paris), low-impact plastics (polyethylene), isolating materials made of recycled paper, natural fibre from flax and hemp which are not treated with pesticides, and so on. The company also takes on normal construction projects, but then tries to introduce improvements, suggesting the use of more ecological materials to the residents or owner. Yet in the coming years Abil expects to specialize exclusively in ecological construction only because the demand for its approach is growing.

Fortes Flavours is a one-man mobile cook enterprise. The cook comes by bicycle and cooks at the clients' home. He works a lot with organic ingredients and prefers to inform his customers about healthy and ecological cooking. The customer and the cook plan the dinner together. In addition to cooking the dinner, the cook does all the shopping, and brings the ingredients to the customer's home.

SUSTAINABILITY EFFECTS OF HOMESERVICES

Now we shall move on to inspect the overall sustainability evaluation of the 215 homeservices selected for evaluation. The evaluation is conducted with the Sustainability Evaluation Tool consisting of 18 indicators and a related five-point ordinal scale for the evaluation of environmental, social and economic sustainability effects presented in the beginning of this chapter. When interpreting the results, it should be kept in mind that boundary conditions for selecting the good-practice services for analysis were that they should be offered to the consumer directly at the premises, and have a positive impact in at least two of the three dimensions of sustainability, compared to the alternative situation where the service does not exist.

The service area scores of the good practise homeservices are presented in Table 5. The indicator scores of all analysed services in each service area were summed up and then divided by the number of services within the respective area. As the effect of the services can only range between –2 and +2, the scaled sum can only range between these values. The scaled sum of all services was calculated by dividing the total score of services throughout all service areas with the number of all services. The formula is:

Scaled score of indicator = Sum of total score of services in each service area per indicator divided by the number of services in each area.

Scoring was conducted by 12 members of the research team. Two experts from each country were involved. They represented the following areas of expertise: environmental engineering and management, environmental policy, environmental accounting, economics and business administration, biology, housing and sociology. Every national research team focused mainly on the respective country's services, but cross-scoring of some services was done in order to test the scoring logic and to eliminate the differences, to the extent possible.

It should be kept in mind that throughout the sustainability dimensions, the scores of the effects are based on this expert assessment. Some may criticize this by arguing that we should have asked the service users about the effects – particularly the social effects — or the relevant economic agents, like the providers, about economic effects like profitability. The latter was realised to a considerable extent, because we interviewed many of the service providers. The former, however, was not possible within the framework of this project. Nevertheless, we did conduct a consumer questionnaire on service use in the project, but although it gave us some additional information on the social and economic effects of the services, it could not be systematically applied in analysing these effects. The main purpose of the questionnaire was to investigate which homeservices consumers already use and which ones they would like to use in the future, if available (see Chapter 3).

Environmental effects of homeservices

The six selected environmental indicators (material use, energy use, water use, waste, emissions and space use) are so called 'pressure' indicators: they are derived from the inputs (materials, energy, water, space) and outputs (emissions and waste) of production and consumption processes, and the effects of these processes on the environment. These indicators can be distinguished from the so-called environmental effects indicators that are used, for instance, in life cycle assessment.

With regard to the environmental dimension, it appears that the largest contribution of the analysed homeservices was to the reduction of emissions, energy use and waste (Table 5). The *emissions indicator* refers to the quantity and characteristics of air and water emissions. Positive effects are related, for instance, to the use of green energy and reductions in energy use and mobility. The emissions indicator has some overlap with the energy indicator, because many measures that reduce energy also reduce air emissions. In all the countries, counselling and information services as well as services within the mobility and delivery area have a major positive effect on emissions reduction. Examples are, for instance, car sharing (less emissions to air), home delivery of groceries by bicycle, and ecological gardening (less emissions to water and soil).

The indicator *energy use* refers to the reduction in the quantity of energy that is used. It also indicates whether a service has an effect on shifting from non-renewable to renewable energy sources. In our analysis, energy use has a relatively high total score, meaning that many good practice homeservices contribute to reduction in energy use. Especially services in the area of counselling and information have a major positive impact. Good practise services for energy reduction in heating, warm water and electricity exist in varied forms in many countries of the sample. For instance the above presented services 'resident as energy expert', 'advisory board on utility costs' and 'EPA energy advice' are relevant examples. Also mobility services score high. Interesting concepts are, for instance, the bicycle taxi and the 'walking bus' services. In the latter service, two volunteer workers of an NGO walk children to and from school every day, instead of their parents having to take them by car.

The relatively high score of the *waste* indicator implies that homeservices can be a good means to improve waste separation and recycling. To give an example, the WBG housing organization in Berlin exchanged the waste containers for mixed household waste for electronic waste sluices that are controlled by a magnetic chip card distributed to the residents. This chip card registers every waste unit of 10 litres that is put into the solar powered sluice and therefore enables an individual pricing according to volume. As recycling is not charged for, residents are motivated to use the waste recycling system. In the neighbourhood where the waste sluices were first tested, the use of recyclable waste systems (for plastic, metal, paper, and organic waste) increased considerably and the mixed waste was reduced by nearly 50 per cent.

It is often argued that a service orientation would substitute products or reduce the need for materials in economic circulation. Contrary to these expectations, the *material use* indicator did not score high in the analysis of sustainability effects. From the consumption perspective, material use and waste are opposite sides of the same coin. If the use of materials is not reduced, waste will be generated. The present findings support some previous studies indicating that it easier to create services for waste treatment than for material or product use efficiency (Aulesbury Vale Waste Reduction in Industry, 2002). The latter would mean intervening into production and consumption patterns, which tends to be much more complicated than dealing with waste issues. Examples of good practice services are car-sharing and joint use of tools. Both in Germany and Finland we found a service concept in which a housing organization and car-sharing company cooperate.

It is noteworthy that the services in the Dutch sample had, in total, a negative impact on material use. In other words they increased the amount of material in the economy, compared to the situation in which the services would not be available. This was because providing many of the services requires additional material use. For instance, services that aim to improve security (e.g. home automation) or to save energy require the installation of additional equipment or insulation. This effect is pronounced in the safety and security category. But also if, for example, an energy consultant recommends a climate installation or additional insulation, extra materials will be needed. In the latter case the increase of materials is, however, compensated by the positive effect on energy use. Another reason for the negative result in the Dutch sample of homeservices is the 'bonus points' system service of one of the Dutch housing organizations. This service scores well on the social and economic indicators because it encourages residents to participate in house activities and simultaneously helps them to save money. However, one form of reward for participation is offering discounts on products at shops (according to bonuses collected). This encourages residents to consume more. To sum up, some of the analysed services had a positive effect on material use because they substitute products or reduce the number of products needed (for instance services that offer joint use of an equipment), whereas the types of services described above result in an increased intake of material in the economic circulation.

The *space use* indicator scored only slightly better than material use. Space use is defined as the amount of space that is used as well as the amount of constructed space used. It also assesses the effect on the quality of green spaces and natural habitats. We were primarily keen on seeing whether it is possible to reduce the need of constructed space for individual use, if housing organizations provide common spaces for certain activities, like multi-use rooms for group gatherings or single-purpose spaces like laundry rooms. Such effects turned out to be minor.

The lowest scoring indicator was *water use*, referring to the quantity of water used and assessing whether the service has an effect on the use of grey or rainwater. It appears that there were hardly any services directed solely at water savings. Services addressing water issues were usually concepts that aimed at improvements in multiple environmental concerns. For instance the 'Resident as energy expert' service is primarily designed for reducing energy consumption, but also water consumption is monitored and saving measures implemented.

With regard to the environmental sustainability effects of the different service areas, supply and disposal as well as counselling and information outweighed the other areas. This was not totally unpredicted because most of the analysed services in the supply and disposal area are directed particularly toward energy efficiency and waste reduction. There were also relatively many counselling concepts aiming at environmental improvements. Mobility and delivery services also had a notable environmental effect, especially with regard to emissions reductions. Services in the leisure activities category were also somewhat significant, contributing particularly to space savings and reduction of emissions. The space saving impact is explained by the fact that the leisure activities group involved a fair number of 'facilitating services' like common rooms for gatherings or playrooms for children, swapping goods like toys, or common spaces for gardening. Someone may wonder how playgrounds or playrooms for children reduce space use. According to the logic applied here, spaces in common use reduce the need for individual space like children's rooms in individual apartments. Likewise, shared rooms for parties or other gatherings reduce the need for larger apartments merely to accommodate for occasional large-scale get-togethers.

There were a couple of interesting repair service concepts. One was a repair and reuse service for household appliances offering a guarantee. Another was a bicycle repair concept in which the mechanic comes to the premises for spring maintenance of the residents' bicycles. But these were exceptional examples and, all in all, the repair services category had a lower environmental sustainability effect than expected. Here, there is an obvious mismatch with the demand, since the survey conducted for this research project indicated that one of the most wanted services in households was a repair service – especially for household appliances – offering house calls. For the time being such services do not appear interesting for the providers, probably largely because of the high labour cost involved. Nevertheless, a partial reason is also information asymmetry – if consumers had easy access to reliable repair services, it is likely that they would be used more often (Halme et al, 2004b). This could have a considerable impact on the durability of goods such as technical household appliances and the like.

We shall now move on to discuss the social sustainability effects of homeservices, and conclude this section with the observation that the overall scores for the environmental indicators are lower than those for the social and economic indicators (Table 5).

Table 5. *Scaled sustainability indicator scores per service area*

		1. Counselling & information	2. Care & supervision	3. Leisure time activities	4. Repairs	5. Mobility & delivery	6. Safety & security	7. Supply & disposal	Scaled sum
Environment	Material use	0.43	0.17	0.09	0.60	0.48	-0.44	0.75	**0.29**
	Energy use	0.79	0.37	0.51	0.40	0.74	0.25	1.60	**0.65**
	Water use	0.49	0.05	0.11	0	0	0.06	0.20	**0.19**
	Waste	0.64	0.35	0.46	0.80	0.55	0.31	1.00	**0.54**
	Emissions	0.90	0.4	0.71	0.40	0.97	0.06	1.05	**0.69**
	Space use	0.39	0.15	0.91	0.20	0.42	-0.13	0.10	**0.34**
	Average environment	**0.60**	**0.25**	**0.47**	**0.40**	**0.53**	**0.02**	**0.78**	
Social	Equity	0.81	0.92	0.60	0.80	0.68	0.50	0.80	**0.77**
	Health	0.63	0.98	0.54	0.20	0.97	0.38	0.30	**0.70**
	Safety and security	0.29	0.58	0.31	0.20	0.13	1.81	0.15	**0.44**
	Comfort	0.69	1.37	1.43	1.20	1.45	1.13	0.70	**1.12**
	Social contacts	0.39	0.57	1.51	0.40	0.19	0.25	0.05	**0.54**
	Empowerment	0.46	0.22	0.91	0.20	0.10	0.06	0.20	**0.36**
	Information and awareness	1.39	0.51	0.94	0.80	0.39	0.06	1.15	**0.84**
	Average social	**0.66**	**0.74**	**0.89**	**0.54**	**0.56**	**0.60**	**0.48**	
Economic	Employment	0.60	1.15	0.54	1.00	0.81	0.50	0.80	**0.79**
	Financial situation of the residents	0.80	0.62	0.8	0.40	0.48	0.06	0.75	**0.65**
	Regional product and service use	0.41	0.45	0.29	0.40	0.58	0.25	0.20	**0.40**
	Profitability for the provider	0.36	0.78	1.06	0.80	0.84	1.25	0.65	**0.73**
	Profitability for the region / community	0.66	0.63	0.4	1.00	0.77	0.69	0.55	**0.63**
	Average economic	**0.58**	**0.73**	**0.66**	**0.69**	**0.67**	**0.56**	**0.57**	

Social effects of homeservices

As to the seven social sustainability effects, the evaluated services had the most striking impact on 'comfort'. The 'information and awareness' indicator received the second highest scores and was followed by 'equity' and 'health' (Table 5).

Comfort refers to the effect of the service on reducing annoyance such as noise, odour, and/or pollution, on helping residents to save time, or on increasing convenience for the residents. Except for the German and Portuguese samples, increased comfort for the residents ranked as the most notable effect of the evaluated services. This is not unexpected – well-designed services do tend to increase convenience and comfort for their users. Yet the finding that comfort exceeds all other indicators should be given due consideration. Services from the areas of mobility and delivery, leisure activities and care and supervision are the ones to contribute most to this social sustainability indicator. Comfort often seems to result from services that save time or trouble for the resident. Fewer focal services actually directly increase 'luxury of life'. Examples of time and trouble saving services are, for example, a repair service consulting at home, a bicycle repairer visiting the building, home delivery or ICT-based information services. This last category includes, for instance, the ELIAS internet market place for over 400 homeservices, which saves the customers' time in searching for reliable service providers. It also includes Info-TV, a building's internal TV-channel that provides information about building and neighbourhood events, tips for energy and water saving measures, and allows parents to monitor the playground of their building from the TV screen (Halme et al, 2004b).

When an increase in comfort results from time saving, it may not only have comfort value (social) for the resident, but also economic significance, at least for those residents whose time has exchange value in the labour market. These instances are, however, recorded separately under the economic indicator '*financial situation of the resident*'.

Services that increase comfort for the residents are provided by both housing organizations and other service providers. For the latter ones the service is usually a core business, and the motivation is the direct income generated. For rental housing organizations, however, the main benefit of the residents' increased comfort is, on the one hand, the tenants' loyalty to remain living in the apartment, thus reducing costs resulting from high resident turnover. On the other hand, due to increased loyalty the tenants can be expected to treat the apartment and common spaces in the building better – an outcome which also saves the housing providers' costs.

Under '*information and awareness*' we assess whether the service increases training, awareness and skills of the residents. It seems that homeservices are a well-suited method for these purposes. Expectedly, counselling and information services contribute most to this aspect. One presumable reason is that many of the new services in the field of household sustainability are consulting and/or information services, in fields such as energy, water and waste questions, or social or financial living issues. The reason for the popularity of the counselling and information format is that, on average, such services engage less personnel than, for instance, care services or repairs.

Equity and health effects appear nearly as significant. '*Equity*' refers to the questions whether the service improves equality between people, whether it helps to combat social exclusion, and whether it promotes fair trade. Not surprisingly, care and supervision as well as counselling and information services score well in terms of their contribution to equity. Care services contribute most to equity. In the German sample there is a special feature vis-à-vis equity. Many homeservices offered by social housing organizations aim at reducing social exclusion by initiating common activities, like providing leisure activities or employment opportunities for youth groups with social problems.

The '*health*' indicator evaluates whether the service contributes to preventing mental or physical illness. As expected, care and supervision services contribute most to health. Somewhat more surprisingly, the mobility and delivery category ranks nearly as high. Good examples are meals-on-wheels, mobile laundry or mobile nurse services. These services allow elderly or disabled people to live at home although they cannot cope with all demands of daily life by themselves. To mention one good ICT-based example, VIVAGO WristCare System is an active personal health monitoring appliance combined with a care service. This service allows the monitoring of the user's health 24 hours a day. During the first four days of use, it studies the user's normal activity level by measuring movement and skin conductivity, and the user's profile is calibrated on this basis. If the system notices a significant change in the user's activity level, it automatically sends an alarm to the recipient – a care service centre or a relative – even when the user is not able to send a manual alarm.

Under the indicator '*social contacts*', we investigate whether the service promotes social self-help like barter shops and swap internet sites, promotes communication in the neighbourhood or improves the neighbourhood atmosphere in general. Services related to communication activities and facilities, like building websites or housing organizations' newspapers, contributed most to the social contacts indicator. These services were mainly offered by housing organizations. Some services may have a negative effect on social contacts. For instance, home delivery may presumably reduce social contacts. Also some ICT-services without any interactive elements can lead to more isolation. A counter-argument is, however, that these services are often used by busy people, who would neither have the time nor the need for extra interaction. In any event, the services we assessed did not have a major effect on social contacts.

'*Safety and security*', together with the '*empowerment*' indicator, score fairly low. Safety and security refers to crime and vandalism prevention in the neighbourhood, and/or to the potential of the service to reduce risk of injuries. Only direct safety and security services have a notable effect. These are services like an emergency service, buildings adapted for disabled people, supervision of common areas like playgrounds or corridors, and a reminder service for medication. One potential conclusion to be drawn from the low score of the 'safety and security' indicator is that even though there are several safety and security services around, only a few have characteristics that make them good-practice services from the sustainability point of view.

Empowerment refers to opportunities to exercise one's own volition and to interact with and influence the world in which one lives (cf. Sen, 1999). In a homeservice context, this refers to issues like improved opportunities for participation, or the provision of new channels for residents toward decision-makers (for instance, electronic ones). We can name a few good examples. In Germany, particularly NGOs play a relevant role in assisting residents to act for their own interests. In Finland and the Netherlands some housing organizations have bonus points programmes for residents who actively participate in house activities. Such programmes aim to empower residents to get involved in their immediate living conditions. Various ICT-based services like residents' websites in Finland and the Netherlands seek to increase channels for resident participation.

In sum it appears that most good-practice household services contribute positively to social sustainability. Since most of the social sustainability indicators applied here relate to quality of life, it can be argued that services have a positive impact on the quality life of residents – even those services that originally were designed from the environmental perspective rather than with social sustainability in mind.

Economic effects of homeservices

The economic indicators refer to the macroeconomic (employment, regional economy, profitability for society) as well as to the microeconomic effects (financial impact on resident and service provider). The highest scoring economic indicator was '*employment*'. The most promising services for creating new jobs are offered by external service providers in the areas of care and supervision, followed by repairs, which is not surprising because both service types are in general labour-intensive. In Austria and Finland good examples of service providers that have a positive impact on the employment of disadvantaged people are social enterprises like R.U.T.Z and T&T, which repair and recycle electrical and electronic equipment. Emaus in Spain operates on a similar basis. They employ disabled people and immigrants, helping them to acquire skills that are applicable outside the supported enterprises.

Some of the evaluated services were specifically designed with the employment effects in mind. To give a few examples, the Big Steps project of the Berlin housing company GSW aims to give adolescents from problematic neighbourhoods vocational training. Craftsmen and social workers coach eight youths to learn a vocation. Practical activities of Big Steps participants include the elimination of graffiti, cleaning jobs, construction works and renovation of GSW apartments – thus, the appearance of their neighbourhood is also simultaneously upgraded. Maunula-Help and Equal Austria, which participate in a European Equal project, follow a slightly similar strategy. They operate in socially problematic neighbourhoods and work together with local government housing organizations. These non-profit organizations offer homeservices like cleaning, small maintenance and running errands, giving jobs to unemployed residents of local government housing organizations.

'*Profitability for the provider*' comes as a close second. With this indicator we assessed not only the profitability of commercial enterprises but also the economic feasibility of the service to non-profit providers, such as housing organizations, NGOs or public providers.

'*Financial situation of the residents*' is an indicator including issues like the residents' ability to save money or create more income as a result of the service. It turned out that the evaluated homeservices had a fairly positive influence on the residents' financial situation. In other words, the assumption that residents can save money through homeservices is realised in quite a few instances. The above mentioned bonus points system for residents is one example. In Finland, the Netherlands and Austria a substantial, although indirect effect on the residents finance could be observed. This effect results from homeservices aimed at reducing resource consumption. Although the service design differs among these countries, the long-term effect – cost savings from reduced energy or water consumption or waste generation – is the same.

Some homeservices like debt counselling by the Berlin social housing company GSW or Info Caravan, a joint service of a few Dutch housing organizations and the municipality of the Hague, have a direct effect on residents' finances. The GSW service is based on a total estimation of the financially strained resident's income and expenses. Economic advice is given on many aspects, including resource and energy consumption. The Info Caravan comes to a neighbourhood with low-income inhabitants on fixed dates. Residents get personal counselling about the housing facilities (energy consumption and reduction), burglary prevention, language courses, information on subsidies for tenants, debt reduction counselling and help in search for a job. Participation rates are higher in comparison to the rates of a normal information desk.

Positive economic effects were not only observed at the provider level, but also the indicator '*profitability for the region/community*' appeared to receive a fairly high score. There is some correlation between this indicator and 'employment'. This is because while homeservices often create jobs or help maintain existing ones, they frequently also contribute positively to the economy of the community or region. It should be pointed out, however, that double scoring was only applied when the regional profitability effect was significant. It is also interesting to contrast this indicator with the lowest-scoring economic indicator '*regional product and service use*'. It seems that the analysed homeservices did not directly support the use of regional products as much as they more indirectly benefited the local community in an economic sense.

Summary of sustainability effects of homeservices

Do services appear to improve sustainability compared to the 'no-service' alternative? We can argue that at least when assessed at a crude level, selected good-practice household services contribute to sustainable development (Table 5; Figure 3). In total the evaluated services contributed most to social sustainability. Comfort, closely followed by information and awareness, were the main sustainability effects resulting from the services. The social effects were followed by two economic effects, employment and profitability to the provider. Even the best-scoring environmental indicators, 'emissions' and 'energy use', scored lower (Figure 3).

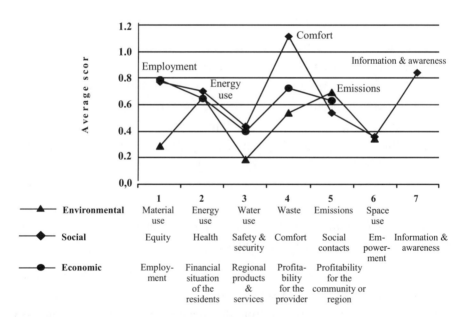

Figure 3. *The relation of ecological, social and economic sustainability indicators*

As most of the social sustainability indicators related to quality of life, it can be argued that a pronounced contribution of the analysed homeservices was to the consumers' quality of life. What can be gathered from this result?

Firstly, it can be argued that services offered directly at home or on the premises improve the quality of life of the residents in general. There is, however, another, more noteworthy argument that can be made. It is based on the fact that all evaluated services are already existing, real life examples, not prototypes or hypothetical concepts. So the observation that social sustainability overrides the ecological effects indicates that the quality of life aspects of the service need to be good in order for the service to succeed in the market. This result is compounded by the fact that many of the selected services were originally environmentally oriented rather than designed with quality of life benefits in mind.

To pick up a specific point, contrary to the assumption that services would reduce material consumption, our results did not imply a major decrease in material use. Thus the result does not support the common assumption that increasing the use of services would reduce the amount of material in the economy. Rather, it leads to the notion that homeservices should be specifically designed with environmental aims in mind in order to reduce the material consumption of households.

What about the service areas? Are services in certain areas more promising from the sustainability perspective in general? No service category appears strikingly influential throughout the three sustainability aspects (Table 5). Perhaps expectedly, some service types are more relevant for environmental sustainability, whereas others contribute more to social and economic sustainability. Supply and disposal, closely followed by counselling and information services, outweighed the other focal service areas with regard to environmental sustainability. This is quite understandable because services aiming at the energy and water conservation and improved waste management are quite common, and in many cases mandatory, in several European countries (Halme et al, 2004b).

Services relating to leisure activities, followed by care services, were the ones that contributed most to social sustainability. It is easier to understand that care services are significant from the social sustainability viewpoint. But the effect of leisure activities, a varied set of services ranging from sports courts to resident newsletters or homepages to get-togethers for residents, is not as obvious. What we can see is that leisure activities have such a considerable impact on the 'social contacts' and 'comfort' indicators that it influences their total significance for social sustainability.

Service areas that contributed the most to the economic indicators in general were care and supervision, and repairs, closely followed by mobility and delivery as well as leisure activities. The fact that both care and repair services have a considerable effect on employment explains a fair part of their economic effect.

One of the main questions that the results provoke is that if homeservices are both comfortable for their users and profitable for their providers, why are they not more wide-spread and more successful in the market? This question will be explored in the remainder of this book, especially in Chapter 5.

3 What conditions the demand for sustainable household services?

Sustainable homeservices are not provided in a vacuum. Multiple factors set the frame for the provision of such services and shape the conditions for their demand and supply. Structural factors such as the housing situation characterize the demand and supply of homeservices in general and sustainable homeservices in particular. In this chapter we first examine the housing situation in the six countries of the sample. By housing situation we refer to issues such as the structure of dwelling ownership and the costs of living and housing in relation to the income level. In addition, socio-cultural features of the cities and towns with regard to homeservices are also briefly discussed.

Consumers' preferences and the national and local service use cultures are another group of factors influencing the willingness to use services. In the second part of this chapter we ask, which homeservices consumers already use, what would they like to use in the future and what they are willing to pay for them. It appears that although the service use habits vary between countries, on the one hand, and between small towns and large cities, on the other, users are more willing to pay for certain homeservice types than others. As a background we use a personal interview-based survey of over 300 consumers conducted in five European countries.

Together these two sections illustrate the macro-economic and socio-cultural determinants as well as the consumer preferences that influence the potential of homeservices to improve the ecological and social sustainability of household consumption.

HOW DOES THE HOUSING SITUATION INFLUENCE HOMESERVICE PROVISION?

The housing situation sets some preconditions for homeservice supply. In this chapter we examine the housing situation in the six countries of the sample. By housing situation we refer to issues such as the structure of dwelling ownership, vacancy rates and the costs of living and housing in relation to the income level.

The supply of services to households, as well as the demand for such services, is determined by a combination of factors. We have analysed these factors separately for each national housing market and the different service areas. As these factors vary not only from one country to another but between different locations in a country, part of the analysis is focused on the selected city and town in each country. The main conclusion that can be drawn is that, although there are few common features in the national housing markets, it is possible to distinguish some characteristics of the housing situation that may eventually influence the provision of services in each locality.

In order to see how certain housing and living factors, such as population size and growth, or building and property structure may influence the supply or demand of homeservices, directly or indirectly, we selected two locations from the focal countries for analysis. Table 6 lists some of these factors. It is quite obvious that large cities consisting predominantly of multi-dwelling buildings call for different forms of service provision than small locations hosting a variety of housing types. However, it is less obvious whether and how, for instance, the relative shares of rented and owned dwellings (tenure status) affects the conditions of homeservice provision. It could also be expected that, for instance, a high rate of vacant dwellings would increase the willingness of housing providers to offer services as one means to attract tenants. The importance of these and other factors for the provision of services to households is discussed in the following subchapters.

Table 6. *Some key features of the housing situation in cities and towns (%, 2000)*

Country / City	Population (2001)	Owner-occupied dwellings	Rented dwellings	Multi dwelling buildings	Buildings with 1 or 2 dwellings	Vacancy rate
Vienna (A)	1,550,123	17	79	94	6	6
Litschau (A)	2,524	90	10	10	90	na
Helsinki (Fin)	559,718	49	47			6.0
Kouvola (Fin)	31,425	61	35			1.4
Berlin (Ger)	3,388,434	23	77	87.7	9.3	8.5
Kleinmachnow (Ger)	17,309	>60	<40	31	69	
Amsterdam (Nl)	735,328	13	87	85	15	~0
Heemstede (Nl)	26,000	63	37	22	78	~0
Lisboa (P)	564,557	48	52	45.7	54.7	13.9
Torres Vedras (P)	16,461	69	31	64.9	35.1	12.7
Bilbao (Es)	349,972	87	10	98	2	8.2
Zarautz (Es)	21,078	88	8	95.7	4.3	0.2

Source: Housing statistics in the European Union 2002 (p34); Hrauda et al. 2004, Jonuschat and Scharp 2004; Kortman et al. 2004; Serrano and Velte 2004; Halme and Anttonen 2004; Trindade et al. 2004

The research carried out in the context of the homeservices project shows that the relative shares of rented and owned dwellings, and the characteristics of the housing stock, including vacancy rates, play an important role for the supply of services. Yet market characteristics, such as the influence of social housing organizations or the size of housing organizations in general, are also decisive.

On the demand side, we perceive that the cost of housing may limit the households' purchasing power on one hand, but also create demand for services that reduce the overall costs of living for the resident. One example of such services are innovative energy services in countries where utility costs are a relevant item in the households' monthly expenses.

Social tendencies in the cities and towns, such as cultural diversification, ageing, or the degradation of certain urban neighbourhoods also exercise an important influence on the demand for services and self-help. Social services are mainly provided by the public administration or to a minor part by non-profit organizations in Finland, Portugal and Spain, while in the large cities of Austria, Germany and the Netherlands, housing organizations have traditionally played a role in the provision of social services to their tenants. Today we can see especially the large housing organizations re-directing their services according to the emerging needs.

Markets dominated by rental housing versus home ownership

The percentage of dwellings available for rent varies from a scarce ten per cent of the total housing stock in Spain to almost 90 per cent in Amsterdam, the capital of the Netherlands. The tenure status determines to a large degree the way the housing market is organized. In Finland, Spain and Portugal, with a high share of owner-occupied flats, condominium associations play a major role in the management of the buildings, while in the rent-dominated markets in Vienna, Amsterdam and Berlin, the most influential players are larger-sized profit-oriented or social housing organizations. The size of the housing organization, as well as their mission, can predispose them towards the provision of a number of services to their clients. This can be seen in examples from Vienna and Berlin, where some social housing organizations take on the provision of services that are mainly provided by public institutions in Southern Europe and in Finland. Apart from balancing prices in the housing market, social housing organizations play a key role in the provision of many social homeservices, as will be discussed in Chapter 4.

Large housing organizations are predominant players in the Netherlands, Germany and Austria, while Finland, with a rather balanced mix of ownership and rent even within individual apartment buildings, takes up an intermediate position. In Spain and Portugal, the construction and sales of private dwellings is largely separated from the management of the buildings, which is either done by the residents themselves or entrusted to a professional housing manager or condominium management company. Also in Finland, most condominium associations have outsourced the housing management to specialised companies and the daily maintenance to maintenance companies.

The tenure status in the local housing markets also influences the availability of common spaces, which is a necessary precondition for some services like swap areas for goods, workshop room for repairing bikes or furniture or the like, or for the building's computer room. Common spaces tend to be more limited in privately owned apartment buildings. Yet, this is not sufficient explanation on its own, because the age of the dwelling stock also affects the differences in space use. In addition, the research carried out in Germany has identified a correlation between the type of housing organization and the amount of common space offered to residents, showing that housing cooperatives tend to pay more attention to such facilities (Jonuschat and Scharp, 2004).

Density of population and multi-dwelling buildings

A second characteristic of the housing stock that influences service supply and demand is the percentage of multi-dwelling buildings, which on average is considerably higher in the cities than in the towns. Apartment buildings, as opposed to semi-detached or single-family houses, offer the possibility to direct a service towards a larger group of clients. The number of dwellings in apartment buildings is closely related to population density – a third factor that influences the supply and demand of services. Yet the relationship between these factors is not always straightforward. On one hand, we find a greater number of suppliers and a greater opportunity for niche markets in the cities, but, on the other hand, we also find a certain undersupply of services in newer neighbourhoods in the outskirts.

Vacancy rates

One variable for the provision of services by housing organization is the level of saturation of the market or certain market segments. This pressure is partly represented by the level of vacancies: the higher the vacancy rate, the greater the inclination of housing providers to offer services aiming to retain residents or attract new residents. In turn, markets that are characterized by an undersupply of housing provide little incentives for housing organizations to diversify their business portfolio.

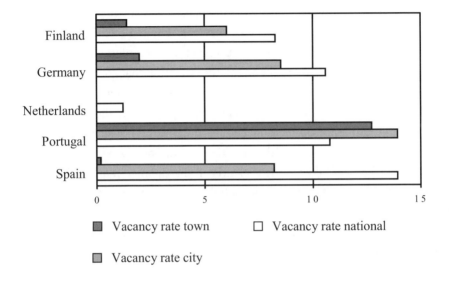

Figure 4. *Vacancy rates (%, 2002)*

As shown in Figure 4, vacancy rates tend to be higher in the cities than in the towns, although some observations regarding national particularities must be considered here: in the case of Spain and Portugal, vacancy rates do not necessarily represent the number of dwellings available for rent and purchase, since a large part of the housing stock is dedicated to second residences or retained for speculation. In turn, the research on the housing situation in Berlin has shown that the surplus of dwellings in the city is one of the drivers for increased service mentality in housing organizations. The situation in Amsterdam and Helsinki is marked by a surplus of larger dwellings, but a scarcity of smaller (and less expensive) ones. Nevertheless, the example of Amsterdam shows us that the vacancy rate alone does not predict the availability of homeservices. Namely, the supply of homeservices in Amsterdam is relatively extensive although the vacancy rate is close to zero.

The cost of housing

The cost of housing and service provision is another fundamental question
that has to be addressed, since it influences the residents' willingness and
possibilities to purchase this type of services. The major difference between
the Southern and the three Central European housing markets covered in this
research project is related to the regulating function that social rental housing
plays in the big cities, Amsterdam, Berlin and Vienna. This function is
virtually non-existent in Portugal and Spain. Naturally, the cost of housing
has a heavy influence on the households' purchasing power and the extent to
which they can make use of the services that are not provided for free. This
negative effect can be seen most clearly in the Spanish market. On the other
hand, financial pressures on households or an increasing percentage of
families with difficulties in making ends meet may induce housing
organizations to offer financial counselling services in order to guarantee
that the rents are paid, as seen in Germany and the Netherlands. Financial
strains on households may also favour intermediaries, which bundle certain
types of services, in order to offer them to the residents at a lower cost.
Examples of this kind of response have been found in the Netherlands, for
instance (Info Caravan service, see Chapter 2).

It is difficult to make an accurate comparison of the rents and purchasing
prices in the different countries, since the actual cost for the proprietor or
resident depends on a long list of variables, such as average income,
subsidies, tax refunds, and mortgage rates (in the case of owner-occupied
dwellings), while rent markets are influenced by regulatory elements such as
frozen or historic rents in Portugal, Spain and Austria. Secondly, housing
prices must be related to the overall income level, in order to estimate its
importance for the family budget.

The European statistics that best capture the influence of housing costs on
the financial situation of households are presented below. They reveal that
the percentage of households for which housing costs represent a burden or
even a heavy financial burden does not reach 25 per cent in the Netherlands,
but is close to 75 per cent in Portugal and Spain. About 60 per cent of all
households in Austria and Germany also consider housing a financial
burden, while the problem is less severe in Finland, where approximately 55

per cent of all households do not suffer financial burdens due to housing costs.

Table 7. *Level of financial burden due to housing costs for households in the different countries (%, 1994, 1997, 2001)*

	1994	1997	2001
Households with heavy financial burden due to housing costs (%)			
EU (15 countries)	20.1	19.3	17.4
Austria	na	11.8	10.2
Finland	na	15.8	11.3
Germany	14.2	15.1	14.2
Netherlands	4.9	5.0	3.1
Portugal	25.9	25.6	23.3
Spain	37.9	31.5	26.2
Households with financial burden due to housing costs (%)			
EU (15 countries)	33.9	35.1	35.8
Austria	na	46.9	49.2
Finland	na	35.1	33.0
Germany	43.3	44.7	44.7
Netherlands	26.5	24.2	20.7
Portugal	45.4	46.1	51.5
Spain	48.5	53.4	57.4
Households without financial burden due to housing costs (%)			
EU (15 countries)	45.9	45.6	46.8
Austria	na	41.4	40.7
Finland	na	49.2	55.7
Germany	42.5	40.2	41.0
Netherlands	68.6	70.9	76.2
Portugal	28.8	28.3	25.2
Spain	13.6	15.1	16.5

Source: Eurostat2004 (http://europa.eu.int/comm/eurostat/newcronos/)

Resource consumption

The analysis of resource consumption in households centres here on energy use, waste and water consumption. From the point of view of the provision of services, it could be assumed that consumption figures may be closely related to the variety and number of services offered by utilities or energy service companies in the form of demand-side management techniques, if the savings potential can be exploited in a win-win situation for both companies and clients.

When considered in the context of housing-related energy costs, the expenditures on electricity, gas and other fuels consumption are highest in Austria, the Netherlands and Germany, representing a little less than four per cent of total household expenditure. These figures are clearly lower in Finland, Spain and Portugal, in the respective order (Table 8). In Spain and Portugal the relatively low electricity and fuels consumption in the housing sector could be explained by climate conditions, whereas in Finland the figure reflects the relatively low price of household electricity.

Table 8. *Cost of electricity, gas and other fuels as percentage of total household expenditure (%, 2001–2002)*

	Utility costs (electricity, gas and other fuels) as % of housing expenditure	
	2001	2002
EU (15 countries)	3.40 (estimate)	na
Austria	3.60	3.39
Finland	1.95	1.96
Germany	4.09	3.89
Netherlands	3.82	3.77
Portugal	2.59	na
Spain	2.15	na

Source: Eurostat 2004 (http://europa.eu.int/comm/eurostat/newcronos/), 2004

These figures seem to correlate well with the greater popularity of homeservices directed toward energy and water savings in the countries where their share of household expenditures is high. In Finland, utility costs represent a smaller share of household expenditure, but for instance the per capita electricity consumption is the highest of the six countries of the sample, nearly 2000 kWh per capita per year (Halme and Anttonen, 2004). Consequently the pressure to reduce energy consumption is apparent. Finland, Germany and the Netherlands have presented several good practice examples of energy counselling or tariff rebates, such as the reduced tariffs for green electricity provided by the housing organization VVO, the energy expert programme for residents organized by Motiva (Centre for Energy Efficiency) in Finland, or the project Amsterdam Reduces CO2 (ARC), which helps debtors to reduce their energy costs by establishing so-called coaching groups for residents (Kortman et al, 2004). These kinds of services are less developed in Spain and Portugal, where expenditures related to energy use are lower.

Energy consumption in households depends on several factors, such as climate conditions, equipment ownership and access to energy services. Households account for approximately 30 per cent of total energy consumption in the EU and, although the overall energy efficiency per household has improved over the last two decades, this has not led to more sustainable consumption levels, due to the growing number of households and the introduction of new, mainly electricity-consuming, appliances (EEA, 2001a). The *EU Barometer on Energy* (European Commission, 2002), as well as analyses by the European Environmental Agency (EEA, 2001b) show that households in Europe are interested in obtaining information on saving energy and that they do purchase energy-efficient appliances, when they have been given information on these issues. These results are in line with the findings of the homeservices project, which indicate that costs are not the only motivation for reducing energy consumption and that environmental considerations and access to information are also important factors that influence household consumption behaviour (see also Dulleck and Kaufmann, 2004).

Water consumption is less dependent on climate and more defined by the size of the household, but the supply situation varies greatly between the countries (Table 9). So, water as a resource is not expensive in Finland because of the good water supply (amount and quality of ground and surface water reservoirs), whereas the Southern parts of Spain are marked by shortage of water (United Nations, 2003). Likewise, the abundance of water supply and the low prices lead to relatively high consumption levels in the Basque Country, Northern Spain.

Table 9. *Water consumption in cities and town (l/inhabitant/day)*

Country	Water Consumption City	Water Consumption Town
Austria	130–150	140
Finland	170	207
Germany	124	114
Netherlands	150	160
Portugal	146	155
Spain	116	178

German figures demonstrate that the efficiency of water usage can be improved considerably by pricing. The average German household consumed 128 litres water daily per person in 2001, which is six litres less than in 1993 and on the same level as 25 years ago (Bundesverband Gas und Wasser, Trinkwasser, 2003). These efficiency improvements are partly induced through pricing: whereas in other European countries, water prices are subsidized (e.g. up to 70% in Italy), German households have to pay an extra charge, the so-called water withdrawal charge.

Saving-oriented tariffs depend, nevertheless, on the individual measurement and billing of water consumption in each household, which is not yet the case in all buildings. Lump sum payment in older buildings can still be found in several cities. Only advanced remote metering will eventually allow the residents to obtain clearer information on their water usage. Such systems are often installed for newer buildings but they are not yet a standard practice for water tariffs in most countries.

Measures to reduce resource consumption can be divided into technical improvements in the dwellings and changes in the daily practices of the households. Apart from environmental reasons, pricing the resources by use is one the most effective means to reduce the consumption. Whereas some charges are fixed by the municipalities (for example chimney-sweeping, street cleaning, ground tax) or the housing organization (house cleaning, gardening, house lighting, insurances, maintenance of elevators, administration), there are possibilities for pricing individual resource consumption by technical measures. New technical measures such as water meters in dwellings, or chip-cards for waste disposal enable the pricing of each resource at the household level and thus change households' behaviour regarding water and electricity consumption or waste reduction.

Home owners can influence resource costs through energy- or water-saving investments. Tenants, however, can only save costs by reducing energy and water usage, which can be supported by an individual pricing of consumption. The dilemma in housing markets with a high percentage of rented buildings is that the investments needed to improve the efficiency of resource use must be financed by the owner, while the residents benefit from reduced consumption costs, since utility costs are generally paid by the household living in the dwelling. So there is little incentive to modernize rental dwellings, especially for private landlords in housing markets with a tight supply situation. The German and Dutch examples show that service providers can actively intervene in this situation by introducing the equipment necessary to control resource consumption.

The best solution for the owner-resident dilemma may be contracting agreements, which place the management of the energy system and the billing in the hands of one provider, so that the economic savings created through increased efficiency can be directed to financing the necessary technical modernization. Some pilot projects for this strategy can be found in the city of Vienna, but in general the only real choice the residents have at the moment in most countries is that of subscribing to a green tariff – at extra cost. In order to further promote energy saving in households, it is nevertheless necessary to set the legal framework properly. This could be done for example by providing subsidies for modernizing the dwellings and designing tariffs in such a way that consumers benefit when their consumption is lower than average.

In the case of waste treatment, individual ecological behaviour depends largely on the possibility (or obligation) to separate recyclable waste. This is nowadays a common practice in all analysed cities, except for plastic waste, which is still mixed with other household waste in some cities. Moreover, services such as the collection, recycling, repairing and reuse of household appliances, such as those provided by R.U.S.Z. in Austria and T&T in Finland enable the reuse of discarded goods, hence increasing resource efficiency and offering employment and business opportunities for small companies.

As a conclusion, the services that not only provide practical information but also affordable solutions to households' heating and other energy needs can have substantial effects on household energy consumption. These services can also create win-win situations for housing organizations and energy service providers alike by creating financial savings for housing organizations. In rental markets, services can help to keep tenants more satisfied. Service providers can find new business opportunities in changing markets. By combining experiences and different forms of service provision, such as resident participation in Finland or outsourced energy performance advice from the Netherlands, new incentives to increase energy efficiency can be created. Moreover, as the good practice examples show, services increasing materials use efficiency such as recycling and re-use services are already feasible and operational on a small scale and are worth looking into and developing in more detail.

SOCIO-CULTURAL FEATURES

When comparing social trends in Europe, we find that basically all countries share common socio-demographic features, such as an increasing number of single-person households, largely consisting of elderly people. What differs between countries is the rhythm of change, since the Southern societies are generally lagging behind, but catching up quickly, as presented graphically in Figure 5. Social change is one of the driving forces for the provision of innovative services. Maintaining and enhancing the ability of people to live independently at home is a key priority in the future. This goal calls for a number of measures that are interesting from the service development viewpoint. Integrating social and health care services under the same umbrella organization is one of the issues under development among service providers. Secondly, housing and housing services are coming into focus in the development of social services.

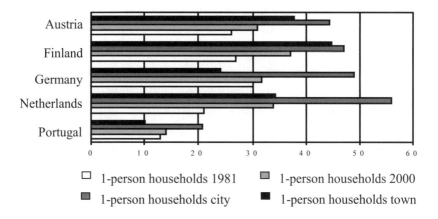

Figure 5. *Evolution of 1-person households (%, 1981 and 2000)*

Within the homeservice project, demographic change, and especially the trend towards single-person households, has been identified as one key driver for service demand, especially in the fields of personal care and social services. In other categories, such as delivery or safety, the demand created by the demographic changes is also visible, but the existing commercial service infrastructure seems to be more developed. The change in the family structures and the growing number of elderly who wish to stay in their own dwelling increases the need for services, which may be provided on a commercial basis to higher-income groups and possibly by non-profit organizations or self-help to lower-income groups. The best-practice examples from the Northern and Central European countries have shown that delivery services for food, medication and laundry, electronic wrist safety systems, service centres and similar innovations, which help to reduce safety concerns and to increase the quality of life, are well received by the residents.

Social polarization

The tendency towards social polarization and degraded neighbourhoods is true for large cities in several countries. In Germany, for instance, the tendency of social polarization is one of the core problems of urban development. Polarizing tendencies in the labour market are characterized by a growing gap between the employed and the unemployed, between high-salaried jobs and underpaid jobs as well as between people with safe jobs and those who work under precarious conditions. Consequently, consumption patterns and lifestyles are polarized as well. These tendencies are reflected in a consequent polarization of housing conditions into social housing districts and middle or upper-class settlements as the increasingly differentiated housing market has enabled solvent residents to abandon stigmatised neighbourhoods. A very similar tendency towards the deterioration of living conditions can be observed in Amsterdam and other Dutch cities. Some districts, which were originally working class areas, are labelled as disadvantaged or deprived and facing multiple social problems: higher unemployment rates, a low education level, poor housing, as well as frequent instances of petty crime. In the case of Amsterdam, a large percentage of the residents exposed to poor liveability, high unemployment rates, potential social isolation, less social cohesion within the districts and qualitatively poorer service provision are of foreign origin (Kortman et al, 2004).

In Central and Northern Europe, social housing has an important function in mitigating conflicts in the neighbourhoods. Housing organizations with a defined social mission often provide services in spite of legal restrictions, which originally limited their activities to their core business. In Germany, social housing organizations are the most important providers of homeservices. The organizations offer, for example, social services as a means to reduce vandalism and improve neighbour relations in buildings with significant social tensions. These services help to counterbalance the tendency towards the creation of socially deprived 'ghettos' and form part of urban renewal strategies for neighbourhoods. The public company Surbisa in Bilbao has a similar function, although it does not directly provide dwellings, but financial assistance to homeowners in the degraded parts of downtown Bilbao. Examples of specific service offers for low-income residents provided by social housing organizations can also be found in Berlin, Vienna and both of the studied Finnish locations. Two Finnish examples, Sato and VVO, show that these kinds of housing organizations may be interested in providing services in order to upgrade their image and attract new customers with higher income levels. The fact that financing problems and legal changes have obliged the social housing organizations to sell a large parts of their flats in recent years in Germany and in the

Netherlands, where social housing companies supply about 60 per cent of the services analysed in this research project, may therefore have a negative effect on service provision by these organizations in the longer term.

Cultural diversity and preferences

Cultural diversity and its effect on residents' preferences are another group of factors influencing service demand and supply in the different cities and towns. Amsterdam, Vienna and Berlin are composed of residents with highly diverse cultural background and this fact is already influencing service supply and demand (Kortman et al, 2004; Hrauda et al, 2004; Jonuschat and Scharp 2004). In contrast, Finland is still a rather homogenous country in terms of people's cultural and ethnic origin: only two per cent are of foreign origin. In Helsinki the figure is slightly higher, 5.1 per cent, but even in Helsinki there is no neighbourhood with a dominating presence of immigrants (Halme and Anttonen, 2004).

Nearly half a million inhabitants of Berlin are foreigners from 184 countries all over the world. About three quarter of them come from other European countries. Nearly a third of all foreign nationalities are Turkish. The cultural diversity has a significant influence of the Berlin economy, as about 13 per cent of all self-employed are foreigners (Industrie- und Handelskammer Berlin, 2002).

Amsterdam is a city with a rather mixed population. People from more than a hundred different countries live in Amsterdam, although most non-western immigrants come from Surinam, Turkey, Morocco and the Netherlands Antilles. The number of districts in Amsterdam in which more than 30 per cent of the population belong to an ethnic minority has increased during the last ten years by approximately 8 per cent, today amounting to a quarter of all districts.

A similar polarization of urban districts has been observed in Vienna, another mixed conglomeration, with a large number of non-EU residents mostly coming from the former Yugoslavian countries or from Turkey. Many of these immigrants live in rather deteriorated parts of the city with badly equipped dwellings. They often have restricted budgets for living, which makes it nearly impossible for them to benefit from any services unless they are free of charge. But many of these families maintain a tradition of mutual help, although they would not see this within a 'homeservice' concept. This observation is also true for the Finnish town of Kouvola, with 2.6 per cent of the inhabitants of foreign origin, mainly from Russia. In the resident interviews it was noticed that they tend to rely more on mutual social self-help than ethnic Finns.

The situation in Bilbao is slightly different, because, in spite of the recent tendency towards immigration from outside Europe, the percentage of the population not born in Spain is still relatively low in Bilbao (3.1 in 2001). Today's immigrants are generally young, of American (<60 per cent) or African (<20 per cent) origin, while Europeans and Asians only represent 18 and 5 per cent, respectively. The three large cities absorb about half of this international migration, which also originates largely from urban areas (Eustat, 2004).

The situation in Portugal is comparable to that described in the Basque Country and is also marked by a rather late start of immigration and a cultural composition that clearly reflects the colonialist past of the country: in the 70s there was a major migration of residents from African colonies to Lisbon and other Portuguese cities, which had a large impact on the composition of the community and also on economic and cultural activities. In recent years there was a significant movement of Brazilians to Lisbon, searching for jobs, mainly in the service sector. Afterwards, immigration from Eastern European countries has started, attracted by jobs in the construction and also in the service sector (INE, 2002; Trindade et al, 2004).

The tendency of ghetto formation in most European cities, in combination with increasing social conflicts and the lessening influence of social housing, could turn out to be an explosive mixture. At the same time, different cultural attitudes related to service provision or self-help may actually lead towards the diversification of service supply, whether commercial or non-commercial. In this sense, the Spanish best-practice service provider Emaus points out that demand for the social services offered by Emaus, especially long-term aid programs, is growing due to the expansion of mental illnesses, family disintegration and a changing social attitude towards poverty, which is now perceived as a minority problem. Social exclusion is increasingly affecting women and people belonging to the age group of 45 to 65, who are offered few services by public institutions. It is also affecting an increasing number of immigrants, who are not allowed to work and make a living, especially not in the professions they were trained for. These immigrants not only suffer from economic shortages, but also from psychological problems due to the loss of self-esteem and alienation, but Emaus' possibilities to intervene are largely restricted by the Spanish Law on Immigration (Serrano and Velte, 2004).

In deprived areas, preferences regarding service provision are different from those observed in higher-income neighbourhoods. Examples such as the Portuguese 'Swap shop of services', Banco de Tempo, show that self-help is more important in these neighbourhoods and may become even more so in the future. The increasing multicultural composition of the European cities will also create a demand for specific services or self-help, and will at the same time require the development of new information and communication strategies, as employed by the Dutch best-practice service provider Information Caravan.

The fact that many immigrants work in the service sector also has an influence on service supply. The first step is to make sure that immigration and tax legislation do not favour a black market in service work. This is likely to prevent innovation and penetration of sustainable services – service offering in the black market is highly unlikely to further ecological and social sustainability, or just economic development. Second, as already exemplified by some of the good-practice services, facilitating the creation of sustainable homeservice offerings would be a good strategy for some non-profit or public sector organizations to apply when they want to integrate immigrants into society and satisfy the demand for particular homeservices.

The above section indicates that there are both similarities and disparities in the housing situation in the analysed countries. It is possible to distinguish some characteristics of the housing situation, which may eventually influence the provision of services in each locality. On the other hand, there are also Europe-wide similarities like the ever more pressing question of taking care of the elderly. What do these findings indicate from the sustainable homeservice point of view? One of the main messages is that in each country there are niches for sustainable services, but they must be tailored according to the existing framework of supply and demand.

WILLINGNESS TO USE AND PAY FOR SUSTAINABLE SERVICES

The previous section gives us some indication about the macro-economic housing issues and socio-cultural determinants that are likely to influence service use within households. But to understand the demand side better we need to get an idea of whether consumers themselves wish to use homeservices and if so, which ones. And furthermore, whether they are willing and able to do so on terms that make the services economically feasible to provide. So far there is little conclusive evidence on sustainable service use. On one hand there are studies on general homeservice use (e.g. Hohm and Wendtland, 2004), and on the other hand studies on eco-efficient service consumption. Both of these streams of literature can be drawn upon, but their findings cannot be directly combined with each other.

Starting with previous findings on homeservice use in general, German evidence based on a questionnaire addressed to 2840 residents living in multi-dwelling buildings of four social housing organizations shows that the most popular homeservices are cleaning of staircases and small repairs (it is typical in Germany that residents clean the staircases themselves). Over 50 per cent of respondents wanted these. The demand for cleaning of staircases is explained by the fact. Multiple home care services for elderly come as the next most wanted service group, even though pensioners were not the dominant respondent group. They were closely followed by reconstruction and refurbishment services. A third of the residents are interested in facilitating constructions to improve quality of life such as internet access, guest apartments, common spaces and sports rooms. Not surprisingly, these were popular especially among younger respondents. Some respondents appear to be interested in laundry service or rental of tools and sports and leisure equipment or gardening equipment (13–22 per cent depending on the service), although the researchers conclude that a difficulty with the applied closed questions method is that more abstract or unknown services like rental of sports equipment could not always be adequately assessed by the respondents, and thus such services might encounter a larger demand if offered (Hohm and Wendtland, 2004). To summarise, the largest interest appears to be toward services that are close to the core of housing: cleaning, repairs, and reconstruction.

Turning to the consumption of eco-efficient services, researchers have typically focused on the acceptability of individual services such as car-sharing, sharing of electric power tools, gardening machinery, and computer resources and washing services (Mont, 2004; Mont and Plepys, 2004; Mejkamp, 2002). There is also some empirical research on the consumption of a wider set of eco-efficient services (Ahlqvist et al, 2004; Behrendt et al, 2003). Ahlqvist et al. (2004) studied the acceptability of 15 eco-efficient service innovations in three Finnish residential neighbourhoods in sparsely populated areas. The following services turned out the most popular: common spaces for hobbies and gatherings, home and child care, space for distance work, and sharing seldom-used equipment. Certain conditions for the use of the wanted services, however, turned up. Expectedly one of the questions was the cost of the service. There was willingness to pay a moderate compensation, but not a high, 'commercial' price. The solution of creating services by combining public, commercial and user input turned out to be a popular idea. For instance, sharing equipment was seen as a financially viable alternative to commercially-based rental, but on the other hand it was thought that maintenance and repair of shared-use equipment is bound to cause problems in the long run if there is no single responsible party.

In a Swedish study on the shared use of power tools and computer resources, based on a questionnaire to 610 consumers, it turned out that that seldom-used power tools would be most appropriate for sharing. On the contrary, consumers are not prepared to rent software, storage space let alone PCs, mainly due to questions of privacy, data security and unfamiliarity of the computer resources rental concepts (Mont and Plepys, 2004).

In addition to the above, studies on environmentally oriented consumption may give some indication about preparedness to use sustainable services. However, it should be kept in mind that although environmental or alternative consumption has been studied quite extensively, the frame of reference is often consumption of environmental or fair trade products, not services (Dake and Thompson, 1999; Thøgersen and Ölander, 2003). Consumers' motivations and requirements pertaining to homeservices differ to some extent from those of using environmentally benign products. Environmentally sound products are mainly chosen with the explicit aim to protect the natural environment, whereas motivations for using sustainable homeservices relate to comfort and convenience of everyday life, or economic benefits (with regard to certain services like energy saving services), environmental aims or any combination of these (Behrendt et al, 2003; Mont and Plepys, 2004; Ahlqvist et al, 2004). The results in Chapter 2 indicate that comfort may well be one of the key factors in successful homeservices, while environmental benefits are more often probably a by-product of homeservice use and thus may not even count in consumer's decision making. Consequently, observations from studies on the consumption of environmental products should be used selectively.

Nevertheless, particularly as regards the 'environmentally conscious' or 'socio-ecologically active' consumer segment that sometimes leads the way to new consumption patterns, it may be worthwhile to take a brief look at findings pertaining to the consumption of environmentally sound products, and see what commonalities they may have with sustainable service use. In essence the question is whether environmentally benign consumption patterns (such as buying green products) are likely to spread into new areas of consumption (using sustainable services). On the one hand there are theories that suggest environment-friendly behaviour has a tendency to 'spill over' into other behavioural domains – for instance from green product choices to the use of sustainably designed services – because of the inner tendency of human beings to act consistently. Other arguments, however, support the view that correlations between different situations or domains are small or even negative. This question has been studied empirically by Thøgersen and Ölander (2003), who found that environmentally benign conduct transfers between behavioural domains, but only in a few of the possible instances and to a modest degree (see also Gatersleben et al, 2002). The stronger the personal norms for environment-friendly behaviour a person holds, the higher the likelihood of spillover. To translate these observations into the context of sustainable homeservice use, the difference between the domains of environmentally labelled products and car- or tool-sharing, for instance, is fairly high. Consequently, it should not be expected that all or even most of the 'green consumers' detected in the product use sphere are ready to use sustainable services. Besides, not all of even the environmentally minded consumers are aware of the environmental benefits of certain services (cf. Ahlqvist et al, 2004). The history of eco-efficient or sustainable service thinking is shorter and environmental effects of services are far more obscure than those of products.

Penetration of sustainable services based on sharing and renting concepts may face more difficulties than products with environmental features. This is partially due to habits and routines, which in fact determine most of our current behaviour, because of the tendency to be consistent with past behaviours (Cialdini, 1988; Hertwich and Katmayr, 2004). Much of our consumption habits and routines are related to the use of owned products and thus it may be difficult to give up owning them. Furthermore, ownership-based consumption is still the prevalent culture, as the major part the economic system is based on the notion of the possession of material goods. Most individuals make their choices based on established social standards. Except for some consumers who construct their identities around environmentally and socially conscious consumerism (Williams and Paddock, 2003), for several people renting and especially sharing are associated with low socio-economic status and personal sacrifice in the freedom to organize one's private life (Mont, 2004). Moreover, for many individuals, owning material goods signifies safety and security, prestige or at least acceptance among one's peer group. To illustrate the point, choosing for instance a washing machine with a class A energy label or a hybrid car are consumption decisions within the prevailing ownership paradigm, and the routine of washing or driving remain unaffected, whereas washing in the building laundrette or sharing a car would indicate subscribing to an entirely different philosophy, sharing. These cultural and habitual characteristics simplify our lives in general and consumption choices in particular. Consequently, the economic arguments of saving money by avoiding the need to buy or maintain a washing machine or a car, let alone the ecological arguments, are often insufficient to change our behaviour in a more sustainable direction.

The above indicates that we know little about consumer preferences regarding household services and service-based lifestyles in general. A number of consumers have at least an attitudinal propensity to use services that could, if correctly designed, enhance household sustainability. Yet there are plenty of reservations regarding which services and at what prices. It takes a fair amount of planning to design sustainable service concepts for households, and more information is needed on consumers' needs and wants to back up such designs.

The European sustainable homeservice questionnaire

In order to deepen our understanding of consumer preferences, we conducted a survey among consumers in five countries. What we detected is that there is demand for multiple homeservices, but that consumers are willing to pay for only certain services. It also appears that the service use cultures vary between the countries of the sample.

We explored which services the residents already use and what they would like to use if available. The goal was not to have an average national sample representative of each country, but rather to get impressions of service use habits and preferences from a set of potential users. Due to the newness and difficulty of the topic, we applied mainly open-ended questions, and interviewed the respondents face-to-face. Without the possibility to explain the concept of homeservices there would have been a risk that the respondents would not really have understood what they were being asked. As a compromise between sample size and interview thoroughness, we decided to interview 50 residents in five cities and 20 residents in five towns. Due to the small sample, in total 333 respondents, the results from this survey should be used carefully and only as an indication of the service mentality in the participating countries.

In all locations except for Helsinki, the interviews were conducted by door-to-door sampling in selected apartment buildings. In Helsinki, the resident surveys were conducted in connection with the spring meetings of three buildings. This sampling strategy was chosen in order to get in touch with the active residents. Before the residents filled in the questionnaire, they were given a ten-minute presentation of the homeservice idea, concentrating on the service examples. The researchers stayed on spot during the questionnaire filling operation so that the residents could ask questions if needed.

It should be noted that in order to avoid answers signalling overly positive attitudes toward sustainable lifestyles, the sustainability aspect was not emphasized in the interviews. Instead, respondents' service use habits and the service preferences regarding the seven focal service areas in general were under attention.

The respondents were mainly adults between 26 and 65 years of age (76 per cent), a slight majority were women (58 per cent) and about half of them lived in the city centre and the rest resided in suburbs. Over 40 per cent of the respondents represented a household constituted by two adults. Most of the respondents rented their dwelling, but the tenure status of respondents varied considerably between the different towns, corresponding largely to that of the general population in the respective locality. In Lisbon and Bilbao the owned dwellings dominated whereas in Vienna and Amsterdam the case was the opposite. In Helsinki the responses were fairly equally divided between tenants and dwelling-owners. The towns in each country mainly followed the same pattern.

A few background questions were asked as closed-ended alternatives. To mention a couple of them before turning to service use preferences, one issue was the respondents' level of satisfaction with their current housing services. Ranked on a five-point scale from very satisfied to very unsatisfied, about half of the respondents reported being satisfied with the housing management (49 per cent), with the services provided at the dwelling (51 per cent) and with the surroundings (43 per cent). About one fifth of them were fairly satisfied with these (20, 22 and 19 per cent respectively), and only a few reported being very unsatisfied.

As to the above discussion about decision criteria regarding product versus service use, respondents were asked to rank four features that they value most in products, on the one hand, and in services, on the other. As to products, quality was the attribute given highest importance, followed by price, convenience and comfort and finally the environmental profile. When it comes to valuing those features in services, the responses followed a similar pattern, except that convenience and comfort were considered a more important element than price.

Which homeservices do consumers already use?

Part of the questionnaire aimed at portraying the homeservices the respondents already use from the seven focal service categories. This part consisted of open-ended questions. For each category, respondents were asked to state up to three services they use and to describe them. The description was important because occasionally the name of a service does not necessarily capture its contents. If the respondent could not spontaneously think of any service from an area, the interviewer probed by giving some examples. This was quite a typical situation, because the name of a service field, let us say counselling and information, does not necessarily connect in a respondent's mind to such daily thing as, for instance, having been instructed by the housing organization how to separate waste.

It should also be mentioned that we were also interested in what might be called 'facilitating construction, such as common rooms or ASDL internet connections. They are of interest in the homeservice context because without their existence certain services are impossible or difficult to deliver, or certain environmentally or socially positive forms of consumer behaviour are deemed complicated. For instance, common space is necessary for swapping goods and workshop rooms for small repairs or bicycle storage rooms make the activity of cycling easier.

In the 333 questionnaires, a total of 2471 services were mentioned. Countries appeared to differ considerably in this respect. Altogether 981 services were mentioned by the Portuguese respondents. This represents nearly 40 per cent of all mentioned services, whereas Finland stands for the other extreme. The 127 services mentioned in the Finnish responses represent only five per cent of the total of 2471 homeservices mentioned. The strikingly low number is particularly influenced by the Helsinki sample. It can be hypothesized that it is not only because of low service use but partially a result of the earlier mentioned interview method, in which the respondents themselves filled in the questionnaire and were not probed by the interviewer.

But the result is also a sign of differences among the service use cultures in the countries. For the Finnish people it is nearly a matter of pride to do many daily tasks oneself – those who use a lot of services are perceived as 'not coping by themselves' or perhaps 'lazy', whereas in Portugal the use of services is a status symbol: households tend to use services if only they can afford them. To give an example, a Finnish family would shy away from telling that they use a cleaning service for the apartment, and if they mention this to anyone, several reasons for resorting to such a service and not cleaning oneself are usually given. The attitude is changing among the younger generations, but is persistent among the age group of over fifty years or so.

The statistical data give some support for this finding. Expenses on repairs and maintenance are highest in the Southern European countries, whereas in Finland they are practically non-existent in the household expenditure structure (Table 10).

Table 10. *Expenditure on repairs and maintenance (% of total household expenditure, 2000)*

	Repairs and maintenance
Austria	1.2
Finland	0.2
Germany	na
Netherlands	1.6
Portugal	2.1
Spain	2.2

Source: Housing Statistics in the European Union 2001

In terms of the number of services mentioned, the other countries fall between Finland and Portugal. Figure 6 depicts the distribution of the mentioned services among the service categories. The majority of the services that respondents reported using fell into the category of care and supervision while the least frequently referred field was safety and security.

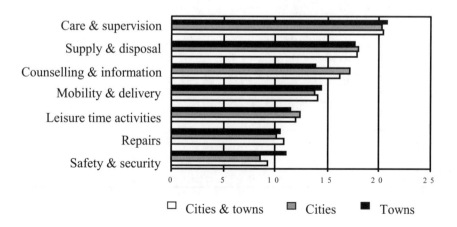

Figure 6. *Services mentioned per service category (%)*

As regards the individual services, hardly any service is dominant in terms of frequency of nominations. They are quite scattered and the frequencies rarely exceed two per cent. Table 11 portrays the service nominations that surpass the two per cent rate of recurrence. No individual service in the categories counselling and information, leisure activities and safety and security exceed this percentage.

The most often-mentioned items include cleaning services and coordinated repair services making home calls. As regards the cleaning services, they refer variably to the common parts of the building or the apartment. Supply of cable/satellite/internet, which represents a facilitating infrastructure was also mentioned by many respondents. From the environmental sustainability perspective it is noteworthy that household appliance repair service provided at the dwelling as well as some waste recycling services are among the often mentioned services. The earlier-cited German study reporting that cleaning of staircases, small repairs, renovations and internet access are among the popular homeservices gives some support to these findings.

Table 11. *Used services mentioned most often (%)*

Service area	No of responses	%
Counselling & information		
Care & supervision (of building, apartment or persons)		
Supply of cable, satellite, and internet	71	2.9
Cleaning service	82	3.3
Leisure time activities		
Repairs		
Co-ordinated repair service	85	3.4
Household appliance repair service making home calls	66	2.7
Mobility & delivery		
Meals on wheels	52	2.1
Safety & security		
Supply & disposal		
Waste collection area for separate containers for recycling	61	2.5
Separate days for collection of old furniture etc. and hazardous waste	69	2.8

Let us next take a look at where the respondents find *information about homeservices*, who *provides the used services* and whether the respondents *pay for services or* resort to services that are *free of charge*. Most of the respondents find the services by simply seeing them in operation. As to the providers, commercial providers supply over forty per cent of used services, followed by public organizations and housing organizations. Regarding willingness to pay, the majority of the mentioned services are paid for, although the city respondents appear to pay for their services somewhat more often than their counterparts from towns (Table 12).

Table 12. *Some characteristics of the services mentioned by the residents (%)*

Characteristics		Cities and Towns	Cities	Towns
Finding the service through...	Direct observation	49	44	60
	Advertisement	35	38	29
	Neighbours and friends	17	18	12
Supplier	Commercial	41	43	36
	Public organization	31	30	33
	Housing organization	21	18	27
Cost of service	Paid	60	65	50
	Free	40	35	50

Are respondents willing to pay for services *delivered to the home or offered on the premises*? In general there is willingness to pay for care services like child and elderly care, repairs or supply and disposal services. Most residents are *not* willing to pay *more* than they already pay for services. However, it was observed that they are willing to pay more for some services that can, when well designed, support sustainability goals. Examples are a coordinated repair services offered directly to the home or on the premises, or a waste collection area for recycling. Apart from that, the German survey showed that residents pay for homeservices that promise savings compared to alternatives, or that offer long-term savings (Hohm and Wendtland, 2004).

Which homeservices would consumers like to have?

We also asked which services the respondents would like to have, but do not yet use (Table 13). The reason for not using the service was not recorded. It may be either unavailability or another reason like high costs. It is noteworthy that the list of 'wished homeservices' includes a fair number of services enhancing environmental sustainability, such as environmental counselling, a variety of repair services that prolong the life of household appliances and equipment, and waste recycling services. But the list of wished services also tells us that consumers could do with care services making their everyday easier: child, elderly and pet care. Also nearby sports facilities and organized activities, as well as security services, were pronounced within the group of desired homeservices.

Table 13. *Services respondents would like to use (%)*

Number of services mentioned: 402	No. of responses	%
Counselling & information		
Counselling on environmental issues and energy conservation	20	5.0
Counselling on appropriate living conditions for the elderly/handicapped	12	3.0
Care & supervision		
Internet connection provided by housing organization	7	1.7
Service for walking dogs	6	1.5
Care for children	16	4.0
Care for elderly	6	1.5
Leisure activities		
Leisure activities for the elderly	5	1.2
Sport facilities and activities	13	3.2
Repairs		
Repair service making house calls (home appliances, bicycles, etc.)	12	3.0
Repair shop for bicycles	6	1.5
Tool rental/loans	6	1.5
Preventive inspections	6	1.5
Coordinated repair service	8	2.0
Safety & security		
Security services	16	4.0
Supply & disposal		
Waste collection area for recycling/ Separate days for collection of waste	16	4.0

There were also some city specifics with regard to the desired homeservices. In Bilbao the interviewed residents desired for a wider range of services in common areas of the building, whereas in both Finnish locations a workshop rooms for small repairs was wished for, and the Viennese respondents on their part yearned for a swimming pool and gym, or storage space for bicycles. Safety and security, on the other hand were pronounced in the responses from Amsterdam. Services like an evacuation plan or fire alarm, video surveillance at the building entrance with display to the apartment, emergency telephones for the elderly and emergency telephones in elevators were mentioned frequently.

Although some of the wanted services support or could support environmental sustainability, others like security services that add to feelings of safety or swimming pools that increase comfort and convenience are not in accord with environmental goals. These are typical instances where different sustainability goals are in contradiction with one another.

SUMMARY OF THE CONDITIONS FOR SUSTAINABLE HOUSEHOLD SERVICE USE

In the first part of this chapter macro-economic and structural housing factors as well as some socio-cultural features were pointed out as partial determinants of household service supply and demand. In accordance with the national housing market it is important to find out the proportion of owned versus rented dwellings, the dominant building structure – multi-dwelling houses versus buildings with one or two dwellings – and the rate of vacancies. These factors provide indications of the relevant actors and the framework under which they must operate. Housing expenditure and the prices of resources like energy and water for their part indicate how much money households on average are able to spend on other than necessary consumption. But also social tendencies in the cities and towns, such as cultural diversification, aging, or the degradation of certain urban neighbourhoods exercise an important influence on the demand for services and self-help. A high population density combined with a dominance of multi-dwelling buildings favour organized service supply in the big cities, whereas in small locations the small number of potential clients can be a significant hindrance for the commercial or public provision of services, and favour social self-help concepts.

The findings obtained on the national and local level confirm that homeservices can be an important element for improving the ecological and social sustainability in cities and towns, although the strategies for introducing and communicating them are highly dependent on the characteristics of each local housing market and even on the specific demand in each neighbourhood.

On the basis of the consumer survey there appears to be demand for homeservices particularly in market niches of care services, small repairs, and services aimed at energy saving and improved waste separation. Consumers are prepared to pay for these services, either because they are not offered for free anyway (care services) or because they promise economic savings in the longer term (energy, waste). An indication that economics can be a pushing factor for a service demand in a certain area is that in those countries where the cost for household expenditure on water, energy and waste are high, the demand for homeservices directed towards water and energy savings or waste prevention is more significant. Additional conditions for willingness to pay are either the dependence on a homeservice or the experience that the service makes everyday life considerably easier in terms of saving time or adding comfort and convenience.

As to the service use preferences, there seem to exist clear differences between the studied countries. On one extreme of our sample there is Portugal, with the highest number of reported services, and on the other extreme there is Finland, with the lowest. The service use cultures in these two countries are quite different. The implication for sustainable service providers and designers is that different services and promotion strategies for various service use cultures are called for. For markets where the culture has a notable 'do it yourself' element like Finland and to some extent Austria, it may be wise to offer services that include a user-participation component (see for instance the 'resident as energy expert' service in Chapter 2), and mediate their use. For the opposite cultures like Portugal and Spain, it might be best to improve the sustainability potential of already existing services. In any event, homeservices are first and foremost social innovations. Like any social innovations, they cannot be pushed from top-down. Rather, they are eventually shaped in a co-evolutionary and interactive process between service providers and users (Dake and Thompson, 1999).

4 Who provides homeservices?

_____

The idea of sustainable homeservices may well be worthwhile, but if it is to be realized, there need to be constituencies interested in providing such services. It is quite typical to assume that new enterprises should appear to provide such services, or to try to persuade large corporations to adopt product-service systems that enhance sustainable development. The reality, however, appears to be more multi-faceted. We observe that sustainable or potentially sustainable household services are already offered by a variety of providers ranging from commercial enterprises or public sector service providers to non-profit organizations. In addition to these providers housing organizations, a previously neglected actor group in the sustainable service discussion, also play a role in homeservice provision. This is due to the fact that housing organizations are in many instances a natural agent to provide homeservices or act as intermediaries for them, because they are in close proximity to the consumers and hence have the opportunity to provide services directly to them. From the consumers' viewpoint, the proximity means that services can be acquired as easily as products fulfilling the same need, which is one of the main conditions for consumers to replace or supplement their product-based consumption with more service-oriented lifestyles.

In the present chapter we discuss the variety of homeservice providers, starting with housing organizations. After housing organizations, the choices and opportunities of the other provider groups – that is commercial enterprises, the public sector and NGOs – will be addressed. At large it is possible to distinguish two main types of housing organizations, namely the social and the profit-oriented ones. This distinction, however, is inadequate especially in markets consisting predominantly of owner-occupied dwellings. In those markets, a few other groups that closely relate to housing and homeservices become relevant. Firstly, condominium associations are legal entities that owners of dwellings of an apartment building or complex must form. They do not themselves provide services, but they can have a considerable influence on sustainability if they take an active approach to promoting and choosing certain services for the residents of their building. Secondly, housing management companies usually manage the housing stock on behalf of condominium associations and thus implement many service solutions in practice. They are also able to influence the decisions of the condominium associations' boards, because the boards usually consist of lay people who tend to trust the professional knowledge of housing managers. Thirdly, building promoters are relevant, particularly in the Southern European context. Although their main activity is to buy and develop building land, construct the building and offer it for purchase, they actually are significant facilitators for energy efficiency and other similar features of the building. Thus in the first part of this chapter we discuss:

- Social housing organizations,
- Profit-oriented housing organizations
- Condominium associations
- Housing management companies
- Building promoters

After the housing sector, we turn the focus to other homeservice providers. The main features of the following broad provider categories will be discussed:

- Commercial homeservice providers
- Public homeservice providers (e.g. municipalities),
- Non-profit homeservice provider (e.g. NGOs)

Since cooperation between several suppliers and the involvement of residents is quite common in the field of homeservices, we subsequently illustrate some typical institutional arrangements of homeservice provision in the final part of the chapter.

HOUSING ORGANIZATIONS AND RELATED ACTORS AS HOMESERVICE PROVIDERS

As mentioned above, social housing organizations are relevant actors in the field of homeservices in rental markets, particularly in some countries, while in housing markets where owner-occupied dwellings dominate, condominium associations and housing management companies as their trustees play key roles. Next these actors are described and thereafter their relation to homeservices is illustrated.

Social housing organizations

Social housing organizations serve the subsidized rental market and therefore mainly relate to residents that cannot afford free market rents. In some countries social housing organizations also provide free market rental housing in addition to social housing. Depending on their funding institutions, social housing organizations can be divided into social or local government housing companies, foundations and cooperatives.

Social housing companies and local government housing

Social housing organizations provide dwellings for people who do not belong to the higher income groups. Some of them have stricter criteria for choosing tenants, for instance based on certain forms of social disadvantage. Generally speaking, social housing companies are present throughout Europe, although their importance differs strongly from country to country. They are significant in the big cities of Germany, Austria and the Netherlands and slightly less so in Finland, whereas they have little relevance in Southern Europe. During recent years, social housing organizations in Finland, Germany, the Netherlands and Austria also gained the possibility to invest in profit-orientated fields like service provision, such as the management of condominiums, or building homes for sale. The functions of local government housing organizations are comparable to those of social housing companies, and they are therefore subsumed under this term.

Housing foundations

Housing foundations are mainly founded by Christian institutions or on the basis of private individuals' donations. As institutions for public utility, they usually address residents with special needs such as handicaps. Housing foundations exist in each of the six countries, but they occupy only small fragments of the housing market.

Cooperatives and similar concepts

The properties owned by co-operatives range from single buildings to whole settlements. The prerequisite to move into cooperative dwellings is to buy a certain cooperative share. Although the shareholders basically have a tenant status, they are involved in important decisions such as those concerning modernization measures. In one sense, residents holding a share in a cooperative lie somewhere between dwelling owners and tenants.

Somewhat similarly to cooperatives, in some countries there exist other forms of housing that are hybrids between social and dwelling-ownership concepts. Right-of-occupancy housing or partly owned dwellings within which residents own part of their dwelling, for instance 15–30 per cent, are examples of such concepts.

Profit-oriented housing organizations

Commercial rental housing organizations exist in all focal countries, but generally only play a minor role in rental housing markets. In contrast, in the European rental housing market most rental apartments are owned by private individuals, who typically govern one or a couple of dwellings. From the homeservice perspective they are a dispersed actor group, which can hardly be addressed. Proprietors of complete building complexes act like a commercial housing companies, whereas individuals owning only one apartment are organized in a condominium association that represents the contact point for the respective tenants. Most commercial housing companies operate in the for-profit housing market. Although free market housing organizations are not under the same legal restrictions as social housing organizations, many of them also tend to follow social aims and goals in order to strengthen their customer relationships. Therefore, their service offerings can also include social or environmental services.

Condominium associations as housing organizations

In the case of apartment owners in multi-dwelling buildings, private individuals are obliged to form a condominium association that is in charge of the building management. They are a legal entity that has the economic responsibility for the respective building or building complex, but they are not expected to create profits. Usually a condominium association contracts the housing management to specialized companies, which are actually the ones that are perhaps more interesting from the homeservice standpoint. Despite their restricted role, here we include condominium associations under the term housing organization.

Housing management companies

Housing managers manage the properties of private individuals and condominium associations. Therefore, the higher the share of private property within the housing market, the more significant the housing management companies are as an actor group. Their duties and tasks vary. Although their duties do not include the liabilities and responsibilities of a proprietor, the roles and duties of housing management companies resemble those of social and profit-oriented housing companies regarding homeservice provision. So, for instance, housing managers and social housing companies must inform residents on housing costs and they could provide similar counselling services on other housing-related issues. From the service perspective the role of a housing management company can vary from only minimal, legally assigned duties like controlling the housing costs to full-house services, including a responsibility for all daily tasks from maintenance to cleaning. In the latter case, however, it is quite typical that a housing management company procures these services from another enterprise, such as a maintenance company or cleaning firm.

Building promoters

Building promoters usually buy and develop building land, raise a building and offer it for purchase. As to services, they predominantly initiate services by providing adequate building facilities and services before the occupation of a dwelling – in contrast to housing managers who provide services for condominium and detached house proprietors throughout the total occupation of a dwelling. As many homes are built and sold by building promoters, they are relevant facilitators for construction decisions that favour or hinder sustainable services during the building's lifetime, such as energy-efficient building facilities. Building promoters seemed to be more significant actors in Portugal and Spain than in the Central and Northern European countries. If the trend for municipalities to outsource part of the design and management of whole neighbourhoods to building promoters or construction companies accelerates, it can be assumed that their significance with regard to service design and provision will further increase in other countries as well.

Who are significant actors and where?

In the previous chapter we concluded that in small towns, owner-occupied dwellings outweigh rental housing in all countries, whereas rental dwellings are more common in big cities than in small locations, except for Spain (Table 6). If we ask which housing sector actors should be informed and influenced in order to promote sustainable homeservice ideas, it could be maintained that social and to some extent profit-oriented housing organizations are more relevant actors especially in the big cities of Austria, Germany and the Netherlands. Thus, relating to their regional importance, building promoters and housing management companies are relevant home-service providers in housing markets dominated by property development and management – namely in Spain, Portugal and in small towns throughout Europe. Consequently, conclusions regarding the relative significance of various housing sector actors as homeservice providers are partially dependent on the country but also on the size of the location (city, town or village).

Still, one cannot deduce the relevant housing sector actors for the provision of homeservices only on the basis of a distinction between owner-occupied and rented dwellings, as for instance rented dwellings include rented condominiums, buildings owned by single individuals and whole building complexes rented by a housing company. The following table therefore additionally presents national rates of private and social rental housing (Housing Statistics in the European Union 2002, p35; Halme and Anttonen, 2004; Hrauda et al, 2004; Jonuschat and Scharp, 2004; Kortman et al, 2004; Serrano and Velte, 2004; Trindade et al, 2004).

Table 14. *Housing stock in the EU by tenure status (%, 1995 and 2001)*

Country	Year	Owner-occupied dwellings	Rented dwellings			Other
			Total	Private	Social	
Germany	1995	38	62	36	26	0
	2002	42	57	39	18	0
Austria	1995	41	45	22	23	14
	2001	56	41	11	30	3
Netherlands	1995	47	53	17	36	0
	2001	52	48	8	40	
Portugal	1995	65	32	28	4	3
Finland	1995	72	25	11	14	3
	2000	58	31	15	16	11
Spain	1995	76	18	16	2	6
	2001	90	10	10	0	0

The rate of owner-occupied dwellings increased in all countries except for Finland since 1995, so there is a common tendency towards property ownership. Consequently, proprietors gain importance as homeservice customers. However, the rental housing organizations are still important for the provision of homeservices, as they represent central institutions for their tenants and are therefore a good agent for the diffusion of homeservices. In fact, social housing organizations actually already offer a wide range of services in Holland, Germany, Austria and Finland, while their service offer is negligible in Spain and Portugal.

WHAT KIND OF BUSINESS ARE HOMESERVICES FOR HOUSING ORGANIZATIONS?

In all countries, a precondition for many housing organizations regarding homeservice supply is that financial investments must be held to a minimum. This is due to the fact that possible margins are minor in the field of homeservices and in general the residents' willingness to pay extra fees is not very high. Therefore, particularly social housing organizations as well as those profit-oriented ones that do not cater for the highest income classes tend to prefer homeservices that do not entail high investment or operating (personnel) costs. In addition, incentives for homeservice provision are based rather on indirect profits for housing organizations such as enhancement of customer relationships, additional external economies and avoidance of social problems. Apart from these similar preconditions for housing organizations in all countries, there are some national particularities for sustainable homeservices provision.

Due to the strong influence of social housing in Germany, cooperation between housing organizations, NPOs (non-profit organizations) and public authorities in the social service fields is quite common. Since the main responsibility for service provision is transferred to the cooperating partner, housing organizations are thus able to intermediate a broad range of services to their residents.

Dutch housing organizations are experimenting with the provision of a wide range of services. In most cases they realize these services in cooperation with commercial service providers. Due to small distances between cities within the Netherlands and a high population density, some service providers such as Lekker Leven began to concentrate on homeservices and provide them nationwide. Finnish social housing organizations appear to be quite interested in increasing their service range by internet and other ICT applications. In Spain and Portugal the homeservice supply by housing actors is so far relatively minimal, but building promoters and housing management companies are starting to recognize market opportunities for homeservices due to the demographic trends such as aging population and changes in social relations such as the diminishing importance of the family as the support network.

These particularities show that the range of services preferred by housing organizations can differ considerably from country to country. In this context, it is important to firstly analyse the local housing market in order to find the optimal homeservice offer that responds to the demands of both the supply and the demand side.

To further understand the potential for a sustainable homeservices, it should be noted that housing organizations are obliged by law to provide certain homeservices, such as maintenance of common technical installations, whereas others involve a deliberate choice. As to the latter ones, some services are closer to the core business (i.e. renting and building apartments and commercial space) of housing organizations, such as counselling on energy and water consumption, whereas others like the provision of mobile laundry service or meals-on-wheels would be considered complementary services from the housing organization's perspective. Service activities related to the core business of housing organizations support usual business activities. In contrast, complementary service offerings basically respond to demands of the residents and therefore contribute only indirectly to the core business through better customer relationships or an increased value of the housing stock. Mandatory services on the other hand are the part of the core business that housing organizations are required to fulfil. As regards enhancing sustainable consumption with homeservices, these service groups are underpinned by a different basis for reasoning and decision-making in the housing organizations. Concerning mandatory services, the question is how to provide them in a more sustainable fashion, whereas regarding complementary services, the question for a housing organization is whether to offer them at all. The closer the potential sustainable homeservice is to the core business of the housing organization (or the housing management company), the easier it is to include into the service palette.

Consequently, mandatory and core business-related services of housing organizations are found in service fields important for the housing organization (safety and security, building care and supervision, supply and disposal), while complementary services relate to all fields privately relevant for residents (personal safety and security, personal care and supervision, mobility and delivery, and repair and renovation). Information and counselling services are mandatory or part of the core business as long as they relate to the immediate housing issues. On the other hand, they are a complementary activity for housing organizations when relating to general issues. Table 15 illustrates these different service fields.

Table 15. *Business types, service fields and service examples*

Business type	Service fields relevant to the business type	Service examples related to the service fields
Mandatory service fields	Information and counselling (on fundamental housing issues) Safety and security (of the building) Repairs (maintenance) Supply and disposal (organization)	Information on legal issues Counselling on housing costs Information on the organization of supply and disposal
Core business service fields	Facility management: Safety and security (of the building); supply and disposal (organization); repairs (maintenance); information and counselling (on general housing issues)	Provision of security services Counselling on reduction of resource consumption
Complementary service fields	Personal services	Local information and counselling on general issues (financial, support for initiatives, entertainment, etc.) Local leisure activities Care for elderly people Meals-on-wheels Repair and renovation services at home Mobile laundry service

Next we will exemplify how to enhance sustainability in the context of these services.

Mandatory services

Regarding construction and maintenance, most mandatory service activities are similar for social housing organizations and commercial housing companies as well as for housing managers and building promoters. Here we highlight some of these services, which are interesting from the sustainability point of view. Namely, the mandatory requirements entail a number of constructions and activities that do not feature as homeservices for residents in the strict sense, but can promote sustainability if fulfilled in a service- and sustainability-oriented way.

For instance, in all countries all types of housing organizations are required by law to guarantee the maintenance of apartments, building environments and technical installations. The duty to maintain all building and apartment facilities is related to service activities such as gardening, maintenance of heating, water and electricity installations and waste management. All of the tasks can support sustainability if the service is delivered with a sustainability-oriented mindset. For instance, if maintenance of apartments involves preventative inspections and the respective repairs, it is more likely that energy and water savings accrue, because faults are noticed early. In addition, landlords and building promoters are generally obliged to provide additional building facilities in multi-dwelling buildings such as parking lots, storage facilities for bikes and strollers, safety applications (evacuation lighting, fire alarm and the like) and additional leisure time facilities such as playgrounds in Germany, Finland and Austria or common courtyards in Finland. To illustrate the point with some simple examples, for instance easy access to bicycle storage rooms and practical design of the room encourage biking. Pleasurable and entertaining design of playgrounds or courtyards not only supports social sustainability (comfort of residents), but it also indirectly reduces the need to travel to further locations to spend one's leisure time – which is often done by car.

Moreover, housing organizations in all countries are required by law to secure the transparency of housing costs. If this service is conducted in a fashion that allows households to monitor their own energy and water consumption and is, moreover, combined with advice on resource savings, environmental sustainability is promoted.

Co-operatives and condominium associations and their respective housing managers must organize regular residents' meetings. Furthermore, Finnish social housing organizations are obliged to organize possibilities for their residents to participate in decision-making, which enhances empowerment of residents.

Core services

In general, service activities related to the core business of housing organizations are closely connected to mandatory activities. However, core business activities surpass basic mandatory activities by relating to housing in a broader sense. Whereas for instance the supply and maintenance of common infrastructure for heating, water and sewage is a mandatory activity of a housing organization, managing additional infrastructure such as internet access, laundrettes, common rooms or residents' garden lots is regarded as part of the core business.

Furthermore, core business service activities of housing organizations are closely connected to the respective housing infrastructure. Therefore, it is often impossible to make clear distinctions between facilitating constructions and service activities. For instance, constructions for additional building facilities (for instance apartments adapted for the elderly or energy-efficient building installations) can be supplemented by appropriate homeservices (such as financial or legal counselling or energy consultation), but are defined as physical preconditions for service provision rather than as actual services. As core business activities mainly complement housing conditions, they concentrate on safety and security services, care and supervision services, energy supply and counselling and information on housing related issues. In all countries, housing organizations or housing management companies have begun to expand their core service activities by additional service offers in order to strengthen customer relationships.

Housing organizations in the Netherlands, Germany and Finland tend to establish subsidiary maintenance companies or to outsource maintenance activities to specialized commercial maintenance companies. This means that other service providers than the housing organizations become more influential actors with regard to service development. In Austria housing organizations set up service centres that provide services for multiple nearby apartments in the neighbourhood, which is yet another solution. The service centre concept is more tied to the neighbourhood whereas the maintenance companies tend to cater for a more physically dispersed clientele.

Complementary services

Service mentality has gained importance in the housing sector during the last years in all countries, and new fields have emerged such as services for the elderly. A few pioneering Finnish, German, Austrian and Dutch housing organizations state that their business has changed from mere dwelling provision to providing 'living arrangements'. Therefore, complementary homeservices span from leisure activities to technical services like renovation services or removal support.

Services that are only distantly related to housing are classified as complementary homeservices, but housing organizations in different countries have somewhat different conceptions about which services are core versus complementary services. In general, complementary homeservices relate to the residents' needs rather than to immediate housing support functions. Services such as facilitating home delivery of products, repair service for household appliances, car-sharing, or mobile laundry service are clearly complementary services. Some of them can, when well organized, enhance more sustainable consumptions models, but their provision requires more changes in the traditional housing organization's mentality than the provision of mandatory or core services in a more sustainable manner does.

Complementary services are furthermore established to respond to social trends such as increasing social disparities or the ageing of society. As particularly social housing organizations face concentrations of old, poor and foreign residents in their building stock, they have started several initiatives to support integrative activities in neighbourhoods. Apart from participating in neighbourhood renewal strategies for all residents, social housing organizations also often establish services exclusively for their residents, for instance debt counselling or computer rooms. Apart from these similarities, housing organizations show different tendencies in each country regarding complementary homeservices.

So, for example in the rental housing dominated markets in the Netherlands and Germany, housing organizations tend to co-operate with local NGOs and commercial and public providers in the provision of social services, such as meals-on-wheels, shopping delivery, visiting services or home care. They have furthermore expanded their range of complementary homeservices during the last years in order to strengthen customer relationships. As a consequence, Dutch and German housing organizations have also begun to found subsidiaries for service provision (e.g. the Dutch company Goed Geregeld or the German company ServiceHaus). In Finland and Austria, local authorities still play a dominant role in public service fields. Therefore, there is less room and need for housing organizations in public service fields like home care or local leisure activity services. Since social housing as well as its service orientation are limited in Portugal and Spain, these kinds of services are outside the housing sphere.

COMMERCIAL, PUBLIC AND NON-PROFIT ORGANIZATIONS AS HOMESERVICE PROVIDERS

Homeservice supply is not only restricted to housing organizations. On the opposite, there are many other service providers that offer a great variety of different services to residents:

- Commercial service providers
- Public service providers (municipality or regional government),
- Non-profit organizations (mostly private, partly subsidized by public authorities)

Actually, similar services are often offered by all of the above three groups. However, they address different types of customers. Generally speaking, commercial providers are interested in the wealthier customer segments, while NGOs or public providers concentrate on the lower income groups. Especially in the Northern and Central European countries, however, the roles of these actors blend, forming a variety of service provision patterns, which we will later address.

Public providers are usually part of the local administration or municipality. Public administration is undergoing decentralization processes in all countries. In one sense this trend means a decrease in services provided directly by the personnel of a public organization, but on the other hand it means that new forms of public-private-partnerships are emerging as the public sector procures more and more services from other providers like firms or non-profit organizations. In the course of this change in the public administration, non-profit organizations have gained more significance as service providers even in the countries where they have not traditionally played a major role. For the purposes of this study, we consider non-profit organizations (NPO) as non-governmental organizations that do not gain profits. Although not part of a public institution, they often receive public subsidies in addition to private funding. Non-profit service providers predominantly do not offer a wide variety of homeservices but rather serve specific fields of public utility such as counselling on social and ecological issues or non-profit leisure activities. In contrast to public or commercial providers, the main characteristic of non-profit service providers is that they are mainly independent from both political decisions and free market conditions.

Finally, a broad range of services are offered by commercial homeservice providers. They appear to be mostly small- and medium-sized enterprises in the social services field, but in other fields like energy provision they are often large companies. In contrast to non-profit providers (NPOs and public authorities), commercial providers focus on specialized services promising financial profits. In the following sections the homeservice offerings of these provider groups are discussed.

Public institutions as homeservice providers

Public institutions concentrate on services that fulfil basic needs, as they are responsible for basic water and energy supply as well as for waste disposal and primary health care. Thus regarding the focal service areas of this book, public providers focus on counselling and information services regarding infrastructures as well as on care and supervision, and supply and disposal services.

Furthermore, we observed that local authorities in all countries have started to outsource more and more service activities to NPOs and commercial service providers. In some countries like the Netherlands, public institutions are not only outsourcing, but also cutting their service provision in general. As a result, for instance Finnish commercial care service providers sell most of their services to the public authorities. Likewise, subcontracting specialized private providers for the provision of public infrastructure is already a common procedure in Spain and Portugal. Consequently, in addition to direct supply, there are two main paths for public institutions to fulfil their public mission. One is to outsource homeservice to NPOs that receive public subsidies. The other option is to outsource service activities to commercial providers, which is the common procedure particularly if the service provision requires specific knowledge or technical equipment.

Thus, it appears that public authorities will in the future increasingly act as a cooperating or funding institution rather than as actual homeservice providers, although they still have a considerable role as a direct service provider in some countries such as Finland and Austria.

Non-profit organizations as homeservice providers

Non-profit organizations are legally bound to social or environmental organizational missions. With regard to their status, non-profit organizations mostly focus on services that demand personal rather than financial or technological resources. More often than not NPO's service offers consist of relatively simple tasks that do not require professional specialization. Consequently, they concentrate on service areas like counselling and information, care and supervision and leisure activities. The following table gives an overview of relevant homeservices provided by NPOs in the surveyed countries:

Table 16. *Main services provided by non-profit organizations*

Counselling and Information	Environmental counselling (on e.g. waste, cleaning detergents & gardening) & counselling on social issues.
Care and supervision	Maintenance of the building (cleaning, gardening) & individual flats. Personal care services for children, elderly, handicapped, as well as health services.
Leisure activities	Social activities for youth and the elderly.
Repairs	Repairs, particularly household appliances.
Mobility and delivery	Home delivery (e.g. organic food, environmentally sound products), shopping assistance
Supply and disposal	Collection of used products such as clothes, furniture & appliances.

Social non-profit organizations perform two separate functions within the homeservice sector. Firstly, as explained, they provide certain social and health services at home, and also organize social and cultural activities for socially disadvantaged groups or try to prevent social exclusion. Secondly, they help these groups to recover social stability through education, special job offers and programs for self-employment. Also some religious communities provide homeservices for disadvantaged groups on a non-profit basis.

Environmental NPOs most typically appear to offer services around counselling concepts, for instance energy counselling. Some of them are specialized in a narrow set of services such as repair and recycling of electronic appliances, whereas the German Grüne Liga or Austrian Umweltberatung offer a wide variety environmental services. Quite often environmental NPOs also try include social goals and vice versa.

Commercial companies as homeservice providers

The spectrum of homeservices offered by commercial providers is rather broad but limited to homeservices that promise financial benefits. Therefore, commercial providers act in generally profitable service fields, for instance health and care services as well as technical services. Nevertheless, homeservices do not appear to be a gold mine for large companies. Most of the commercial companies in the real estate and traditional homeservice field are fairly small companies. For instance, the Finnish business register states that 85 per cent of all Finnish real estate service providers and 76 per cent of all homeservice providers have less than five employees (Statistics Finland, 2001). In order to gain customers, they consequently usually compete with other small providers in fulfilling customer demands. In all countries, this results in two different strategies: specialization and diversification of the service offer.

Commercial service providers choose a strategy of specializing their service offer particularly in markets with a demand for highly sophisticated services, which predominantly exist in big cities. Apart from that, some homeservices such as technical services or particularly health services demand a certain specialized know-how as well as specific technical equipment. These service providers may also operate on the regional level in order to serve less densely populated areas as well.

In contrast, some commercial homeservice providers have not specialized but generalized their service portfolio in order to provide service packages on a broader spatial level. An example of a generalist service provider is the Dutch company Lekker Leven, a subsidiary of the de Key housing organization, which mediates a wide set of homeservices in multiple locations in the Netherlands. Lekker Leven does not provide all services with its own personnel but involves local providers. However, Lekker Leven is only able to act nationwide because of the extraordinarily dense population throughout the whole country in the Netherlands.

ALONE OR IN COOPERATION? ARRANGEMENTS FOR HOMESERVICE PROVISION

Residents may obtain homeservices through a number of different kinds of arrangements. Based on the observation that housing organizations could be a natural agent offering or mediating the provision of services directly to the resident's home, we will next turn to examining alternative ways of supplying homeservices. Hence 'living in a dwelling' would become the point of reference. It should be noted that the following discussion relates to other forms of dwellings than single-family housing. With that restriction in mind, a number of ways for service provision may be identified (cf. Hohm et al., 2002) (Figure 7). However, most of the options for service supply involve the housing organization in one way or the other. We can recognize three main options in which the housing organization is involved: direct provision by the housing organization, cooperation with other providers, and resident involvement. All of these have two sub-variations. On the other hand, other, 'external' service providers may supply the service directly to the resident independently of the housing organization. The latter instance – other service providers than housing organizations offering homeservices directly without any links to the housing organization – is not discussed in detail here.

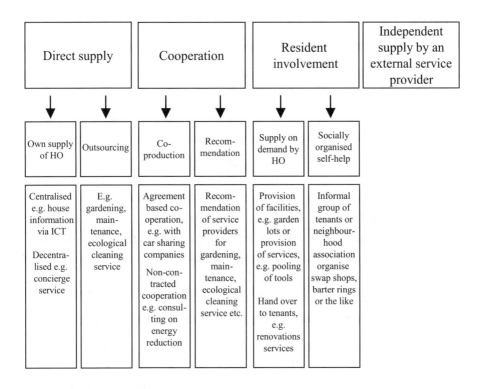

Figure 7. *Options for the supply of homeservices*

Direct provision

The direct provision option means that the service provider is the housing organization itself (e.g. a condominium association, a social or profit-oriented rental housing provider). A variation of direct supply is the option where the housing organization buys the service from an external service provider (e.g. outsourced gardening, cleaning, etc.). Actually, condominium associations tend to outsource the provision of all or nearly all services, because they are only legal entities formed by the residents who own the apartments in the respective building. Social or profit-oriented rental housing organizations, on the other hand, tend to supply directly services that they consider as their core business and that do not require extra personnel or financial investments. But also for them, outsourcing is an increasingly common arrangement for service supply, including basic services such as maintenance or building cleaning. Nevertheless, from the residents' perspective, the outsourced service is experienced as basically similar to one provided by the housing organization's own personnel.

Cooperation

The housing organization may also choose to cooperate with the service provider. For instance, residents of the housing organization may get a discount price for membership in a car-sharing organization: the housing organization provides the parking space for shared cars, and assists in the key exchange unless the car locks operate with mobile phones as in the Finnish CityCarClub. This arrangement is usually contract-based, and could be termed *co-production*. A looser institutional arrangement is sufficient if the housing organization acts as an intermediary between the residents and the service provider, for instance by *recommending* a certain service provider (e.g. a plumber) or by taking over a transaction on behalf of the service provider (e.g. a janitor selling tickets to public transport).

Housing organizations particularly in the Netherlands, Germany and Austria have already begun to use the provision of various homeservices as a marketing instrument to support customer relationships. Examples of homeservices provided through cooperation are gardening services or additional help for elderly residents. Different customer segments are obviously interesting for different cooperating service providers. NPOs or the public sector are generally the partners when the focal residents cannot afford to pay for the services, whereas for wealthier customer segments, commercial providers are the natural partners. Also the service offer for the different customer groups varies somewhat. Housing organizations are often the initiating agents for cooperation, but for several service enterprises a good marketing strategy would be to actively approach the housing organizations as a channel for facilitating their service offer, be it by recommendation or contract-based cooperation.

Whether the homeservices are directly supplied or offered via cooperative arrangements, a crucial success factor for the homeservice offer is that residents have an easy and flexible access to the service. Homeservice provision demands a central contact and information point for the residents – a janitor or concierge, a service centre, or web presence. Janitors are usually preferred by the residents, but housing organizations in most of the surveyed countries have mainly discontinued this service, Austria as the latest one. In Germany concierges or janitors still partly play the role of central contact person in the rental housing sector. To give another example, the housing organization Harlacherweg in Vienna established a local service centre serving 800 dwellings in order to be present on site.

In Finland and the Netherlands internet use is widespread and therefore the web is increasingly being used in homeservice provision. In the Netherlands, for instance, the commercial service provider Lekker Leven concentrates only on the provision of homeservices and promotes its range of services nationwide via the internet, although most of the contacts coming from customers are made by phone. In Finland two largest nation-wide social housing organizations, VVO and Sato, are increasingly developing web solutions to improve the flexible availability of their services.

What were the common institutional arrangements found in the practical applications of sustainable homeservices? As Figure 8 shows, nearly 20 per cent of the evaluated good-practice sustainable homeservices are provided in cooperative arrangements by two or more providers:

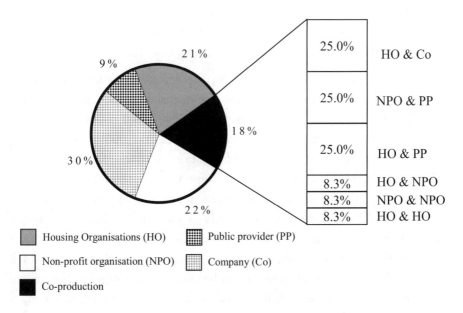

Figure 8. *Division of the providers of the evaluated sustainable homeservices (%)*

The largest single provider group were commercial enterprises (30 per cent), followed by non-profit organizations and housing organizations, amounting to about one-fifth each. Public sector providers were the smallest provider group, if we look at homeservices offered by one single provider. Their range of offerings is, however, larger with regard to homeservices that are provided in cooperation with another provider or providers. Actually it appears that public sector organizations were often initiators of homeservices that are offered by multiple providers together. Also the role of social housing organizations in cooperative arrangements is considerable whereas that of commercial enterprises and NPOs is smaller.

Residents' involvement

In all of the alternatives outlined above, the residents assume a typical customer role in the sense that they do not participate in the production of the service. There is, however, yet another service model: the resident participates in the actual creation of the service. Some services, such as organizing house parties or pooling tools lend themselves better for resident involvement than others. Often these activities are not even called 'services', but can still be considered within the broad group of homeservices, because they fulfil certain customer needs.

In the resident involvement case the service can be organized so that the housing organization provides the necessary material component of a service and the residents do the work themselves. The material component can be durable and shared successively by the residents (e.g. pooling tools), or it can be a single-use good (provision of paint or other renovation materials). This can be called a 'supply on demand' option (e.g. of tools or renovation materials). Finally, there is an option in which the residents themselves create the service informally, as socially organized self-help (e.g. barter rings, in-house flea-markets, informal tenants' meetings, neighbourhood association). In this case, the housing organization may have a role as a space provider. The initiator may be either the housing organization or the active residents. The latter kind of concept, however, requires a certain willingness to socialize with one's neighbours. We addressed this issue in the resident survey, and it turned out that the majority of the respondents only meet their neighbours 'by chance' (54 per cent). The most frequently mentioned instance for meeting neighbours were annual or bi-annual condominium association or tenant meetings (38 per cent).

Involvement of residents is more common for social housing organizations, because the financial resources of their residents are more restricted. This was reflected especially in the homeservices analysed in Berlin, because the sample involved quite a few social sustainability oriented services that aim primarily to improve the life of disadvantaged residents and the surroundings in less well-to-do neighbourhoods. Still, also condominium associations apply resident (dwelling owner) engagement for some tasks like spring and autumn preparation of the house garden, at least in some countries. But there has to be an organizing party, which most naturally would be the housing manager. This indicates that within property-dominated markets, housing managers could play an increasing role in initiating mutual aid in the future.

SUMMARY OF HOMESERVICE PROVIDERS AND THEIR OFFERINGS

Often when thinking about sustainable services, we tend to assume that new enterprises should miraculously appear to provide such services, or try to persuade large corporations to adopt product-service systems that enhance sustainable development. The findings of this research project, however, reveal a somewhat more multifaceted picture of the potential or most prominent providers of homeservices. We observe that sustainable or potentially sustainable household services are offered by a variety of providers from commercial enterprises or public sector service providers to non-profits and housing organizations.

The division of labour between the different actors offering household services varies to a greater or lesser extent between the countries. One of the sources of variation with regard to the provision of homeservices is the legislation regarding the duties of different actors, for instance the public sector or the housing organizations. These largely determine the need and the niche for other service providers. The relative importance of homeservice providers also varies between locations. In the big cities of Austria, Germany and the Netherlands, social housing organizations offer a large number of dwellings and a variety of homeservices, whereas in the Southern European countries and in the small towns in all the studied countries there are more privately owned apartments, and consequently housing management companies are the key actors in the housing sector. In the Portuguese and Spanish housing markets building promoters also bear significance with regard to homeservice provision. These housing related organizations, however, do not have the competence and capacity to provide many services. They have certain core business areas, within which they have expertise, and services that directly relate to their core business are the most obvious ones for housing organizations or housing management companies to offer. However, there is a variety of other homeservices that customers may want or need. In these instances other providers, such as commercial enterprises, NPOs or public sector organizations, are appropriate providers.

About one-fifth of the good-practice sustainable homeservice examples evaluated for this book are provided in cooperation by two or more actors (Figure 8). Housing organizations are partners in the majority of these cooperations. Housing organizations could, however, be utilized much more often as a marketing channel for a variety of homeservices provided by, for instance, small- and medium-sized service enterprises. This would solve one of their main problems: lack of marketing resources to spend on informing potential customers about their service offering. Designers and providers of (sustainable) homeservices could also more often make use of housing organizations, but many times mutual benefits remain undiscovered, because housing organizations are not a usual business partner for other service providers.

Nevertheless, the mere provision of homeservices does not necessarily mean anything in terms of sustainability. It is one question to offer homeservices, and yet another to offer them in such a form that the sustainability of household consumption is enhanced. In this regard the service providers have two options. They can either provide their existing services in a more sustainable way, or they can start to develop new, sustainable service offerings. For housing organizations and housing management companies, it is easier to start making their mandatory or core services more sustainable than to begin to offer totally new services that are more distant from their core business. For instance, housing organizations are responsible for certain technical facilities like the plumbing and radiators of the building's dwellings. It is a smaller step to offer, for instance, preventative inspections of these facilities and repair service for the early correction of faults in order to prevent water and heating energy losses than to start offering, for instance, meals-on-wheels to the residents. As regards new complementary homeservices promoting sustainability, housing organizations prefer to set up subsidiaries (a typical strategy in the Netherlands for instance) or cooperate with other service providers.

Competition in the housing market is increasing. For housing organizations there are various ways to meet the competitive challenge. One of them is to develop a strategy to offer more (sustainable) homeservices. Homeservices increase customer satisfaction and the improved image can make the housing provider more attractive in the eyes of existing and potential residents. Consequently it enables longer tenancies and thus reduces the changeover of residents. It reduces costs because happier tenants are inclined to treat the property better. Furthermore, better service offerings may attract better-income tenants. Thus the main motivation for housing organizations to offer homeservices is not the direct extra income generated. Often the benefits of these services are indirect. Thinking beyond immediate business benefits, a service orientation is one practical ways of taking responsibility beyond company interests with respect to residents and society.

Public, non-profit and commercial organizations have varied roles as homeservice providers. Public authorities are required to provide public transport, energy and water supply, leisure time and social infrastructure as well as certain social services. In all countries, the homeservice market is presently undergoing a change process due to decentralization strategies of public institutions. While in the past decades public providers tended to produce most of the services themselves, they have recently begun to outsource services to or cooperate with NPOs and commercial service providers. Hence subcontracting specialized private providers for initially public services is already a common procedure in all countries. Therefore, public authorities increasingly act as the funding or cooperating institution in the provision of homeservices.

For NPOs, homeservices are a practical way to promote sustainable development. NPOs mainly focus their activity on labour-intensive tasks that are useful for society. Main actors in the non-profit homeservice sector are environmental associations, welfare organizations and urban renewal initiatives. While welfare institutions provide social services for special groups such as young, elderly, disabled or disadvantaged residents, environmental associations counsel residents on diverse ecological subjects regarding caring for the local environment, nutrition and sustainable consumer behaviour. Urban renewal initiatives concentrate on a certain area and provide a broad range of community activities such as mediation, debt counselling or resident participation. Non-profit organizations are important actors for the dissemination of sustainable homeservices because they have either a social or an environmental mission in their service provision. We also found examples of NPOs providing services in which social and environmental aims were intertwined.

The commercial homeservice market is characterized by either specialization or diversification strategies. This leads to all-round service companies, on the one hand, and to professional specialists in a single service, on the other. Commercial companies mainly specialize in service fields that require a specific knowledge or technical equipment. In contrast, generalized companies provide a wide range of services, including social, technical and counselling services.

To conclude, the good practice sustainable household services seem to be fairly equally provided by many kinds of organizations from private enterprises to non-profit and housing organizations, and public providers. This finding bears significance particularly for the eco-efficient product-service systems community within which it is often at least implicitly assumed that corporations should be the leading agents in sustainable consumer service provision (Vercalsteren and Gerken, 2004; Tischner and Verkuijl, 2002). Yet less than 30 per cent of the sustainable homeservices evaluated here were provided by commercial firms and, moreover, most of them were small or medium-sized. NPOs and housing organizations provided 20 per cent of services each. On the top of that, another 20 per cent of the evaluated homeservices were co-produced, mainly by two partners or in a couple of cases even more. Public providers and housing organizations were the providers that most often seemed to co-operate with other constituencies in homeservice production. This implies that the provision of sustainable services to households is a multi-faceted arena, where the importance of various actors and forms of their cooperation should be given appropriate attention in order to come up with feasible service propositions.

5 Drivers and hindrances for sustainable homeservices

The evaluation of different household services in Chapter 2 showed that well-designed homeservices can have many benefits, such as comfort to their users, economically feasible activity for their providers, and environmental benefits to society. However, sustainable homeservices are still an uncommon form of consumption and a marginal business activity. Hence the questions arise: why are homeservices not more widespread, even though they appear comfortable and profitable? Why are the good features of sustainable services not a sufficient condition to ensure their breakthrough in the market? And furthermore, what trends support the penetration of sustainable household services and how could they be utilized?

The potential improvement in the quality of life that homeservice use could bring about may often remain unseen by the consumers, because ownership-based consumption is still the prevalent culture. Much of daily life is organized around behaviour patterns that involve the possession of material goods, and it may be complicated to break such patterns even if one sees the benefits of service use (see Chapter 3 for further discussion).

Turning to the profitability question, we defined the profitability of the service to the provider as profitability in the long term (be the provider a private enterprise, NGO or public organization) or the improvement of the economic efficiency of the whole service system. Even if a service is profitable in the long term, this may still be in contradiction with the ability of the service to generate profits in the short term – an ideal that often governs present economic thinking. Likewise, the economic efficiency of the system is seldom the focus of optimisation today. Rather, single and occasionally very small units – even within a single organization – focus on their own immediate profitability. Even if it is understood that it stands against the best possible economic outcome for the whole system, each unit is judged by the achievement of its own goals and thus keeps pursuing them. For instance, some housing organizations have realized that offering homeservices increases tenant satisfaction and loyalty, leading to longer tenancies and reduced vandalism or negligence. This indirect outcome of homeservices saves overall costs, and therefore justifies their provision. However, the culture of many housing organizations is still guided by the assumption that their business is to provide only the dwelling. If exposed to homeservice ideas, such organizations tend to see them as additional costs – unless the tenants directly pay for them. Indirect or long-term economic benefits are thus disregarded.

Yet another point is that the current infrastructures and market incentives often favour the ownership of goods, and it is not easy to find actors with an interest in changing these structures. Producers, who in some sense would be in a good position to initiate changes such as designing more durable goods and combining them with repair and maintenance services, find the concept very threatening because they mainly operate under the totally opposite paradigm of selling as many products as possible at as low a price as possible. Over the years this paradigm has led to increasingly short product lifetimes. Besides, would a producer be willing to test a different marketing strategy, it would often face the need to break the borders of the present supply chain, as well as create different system for generating profits. For instance, washing machine manufacturers might need to co-operate with housing organizations if they aim to create a washing service business instead of selling machines for single household use only.

But there are other developments that can support the supply and demand for services. For instance, the internet as a communication channel allows smaller service providers to inform potential customers about their offering at a low cost, or create totally new service concepts utilizing the internet. Even more so, the Europe-wide growth in the number of elderly wanting to continue living at home for as long as possible is an undisputed opportunity for homeservices. The increasing demand for more comfort at home among many potential customer groups from wealthy singles to working families with small children is yet another trend which can at best enhance more service-oriented lifestyles. However, this is not to say that service-orientation automatically leads to more sustainable ways of consumption. In order to do so, homeservices must be designed with sustainability aspects in mind.

In sum, when planning or designing such services, it is good to keep in mind that there are certain incentives that can be made use of and, on the other hand, obstacles that need to be dodged. These will be discussed in the present chapter. Some of the promoting factors and obstacles relate to homeservices in general and others particularly to sustainable homeservices. They stem from many different sources. We have divided the promoting factors and hindrances into four categories. The first three loosely follow the sources of isomorphic change outlined by DiMaggio and Powell (1991). These are legislation, market or customer factors, and industry norms. In addition, there are factors that relate to physical infrastructures, which we will discuss separately. These factors are partially intertwined. For instance, legislation concerning housing and homeservices influences the industry norms and some conditions of demand. Yet it is helpful to scrutinize the factors separately. There are both similarities and differences in these factors between countries, mainly due to variations in the institutional setting of housing and the different service use cultures in these different countries.

LEGISLATION AND REGULATION

In this section we will concentrate on four general issues: taxation, public subsidies, labour market legislation, and government employment policies. There would be many others, but we prefer to introduce the ones that were evident throughout the focal countries.

Taxation and indirect labour costs

One of the main obstacles for using homeservices is their cost. In general, households would be willing to pay less for services than the price at which they can be provided (Varjonen, Aalto and Leskinen 2005). In this respect taxation and indirect labour costs become a significant question. For instance, high indirect labour costs were considered an obstacle to the use of labour-intensive homeservices in Austria, the Netherlands, Finland, and to some extent in Germany. In Austria, Finland and the Netherlands these costs add about 50 per cent to the employee's salary. In Germany the respective figure is 44 per cent, which is paid half by the employer and half by the employee. On the other hand, in Portugal these costs add only around 22 per cent, consisting of indirect costs related to social security (19 per cent), vocational training (0.5 per cent) and other social costs that account for the remaining two per cent. Taxation may also come into play in another way: some service workers may be unwilling to work, if their already low salary is taxed rather heavily, and if they have the alternative of getting social security benefits that are equal or nearly equal to their net salary.

To alleviate this problem, a tax deduction scheme for homeservices was recently introduced in Finland (in 2000) and Germany (in 2003). In Finland households can deduct 60 per cent of the costs of homeservices they have used. The maximum deduction is 1150 euros per spouse (in families). In order to get the deduction households have to use a registered service provider. Households can also deduct the indirect labour costs for an employee, if they have paid salary and both the direct and indirect labour costs of that employee, provided that the work is done either at the employer's home or summer cottage. Tax-deductible services are home assistance, repair and care services, shopping assistance, cleaning and child-care (Finnish Tax Administration, 2005). In Germany the set of deductible homeservices is smaller. Only 'simple homeservices' that buyers could actually perform themselves (for instance gardening, apartment cleaning, simple renovation) are tax deductible, whereas professional services like tiling, electrical installations and so on are excluded (§ 35a, German Income Tax Law). An individual can deduct 25 per cent of the costs of the homeservice and get a tax return of up to 600 €. The main motivation for the Finnish deduction system was to promote service employment in general, whereas in Germany the main target has been the employment of unskilled workers and the reduction of black-market labour. In Finland the tax deduction opportunity has clearly increased the use of homeservices in households (Varjonen et al, 2005; Niilola et al. 2005), whereas from

Germany there is so far little evidence about the effects of the legislation since it was introduced only recently.

Subsidies

Public subsidies are a multifaceted issue with regard to sustainable homeservices. In some countries like Denmark households can receive subsidies compensating part of the costs of homeservices used. The eventual outcome is rather similar to tax deduction. In Denmark this form of subsidizing has increased the use homeservices considerably, but in some other countries, which have experimented with somewhat similar systems, the results have not been positive (Varjonen et al, 2005). As regards homeservices with particular social or environmental effects, subsidies are available, for instance, for a variety of social purposes and energy efficiency.

To give a few examples of the energy efficiency subsidies, there are a number of subsidies concerning energy screening and investments for energy efficiency improvements of the building. In Austria, Finland, Germany and the Netherlands there are several types of energy efficiency subsidies available, both for screening and for installing energy saving facilities. In the southern countries of the sample, subsidies for energy efficiency do not appear to include services but only physical structures. For example in Portugal solar energy equipment is a tax deductible cost, and in some regions in Spain public subsidies are available for ecological renovations of buildings.

Voluntary energy conservation agreements for the housing sector in Finland are expected to encourage housing organizations to provide ecologically sustainable homeservices. The agreements cover 290.000 apartments, which is over 65 per cent of the total social housing organizations' dwelling stock (Ministry of the Environment, 2002). It is expected that the objectives – to decrease heating energy and water consumption from 1998 levels by 10 per cent by the year 2008 from and 15 per cent by the year 2012 – cannot be achieved just by applying new construction measures at the building phase, but that the target also demands other services such as facilities management and changing the daily routines of the residents.

Labour market legislation and government employment policies

In some countries like Austria and Finland there are particular government employment policies aiming at job creation for the unemployed that can contribute to homeservice provision. In Portugal, the government employment policy promotes homeservices in an indirect way. Public organizations promote professional training and the creation of new business by unemployed persons, and thereby stimulate the emergence of very small enterprises, which typically provide homeservices such as personal transportation or cleaning. These enterprises receive subsidies for the start-up costs, including new material acquisitions. Furthermore, in Portugal there is a special tax deduction for unskilled workers offering homeservices such as home cleaning or child sitting.

In several European countries there are social enterprises or co-operatives, which aim to create work for people with disabilities. These organizations are foreseen to become agents that could, among other things, provide labour-intensive homeservices that do not require advanced technical skills. However, in many countries this legislation and enterprise form is relatively new, and therefore there is fairly little practical experience of social enterprises as a means of providing homeservices. Legislation regarding social enterprises varies between countries, but the basic idea is that a certain percentage of the employees of social enterprises are disadvantaged people such as long-term unemployed, immigrants or disabled people. Governments support the salaries of the persons hired on social grounds for 1–3 years. Apart from this, social enterprises are generally expected to be economically self-sufficient. The principal idea is that social enterprises provide their disadvantaged employees with skills that allow them to enter the normal job market later on (CEFEC, 2005). The earlier introduced service providers RUTZ and T&T are examples of such enterprises (Chapter 2). Also some EQUAL projects funded by the European Social Fund apply the idea that homeservices like cleaning, running errands and shopping assistance are 'locally produced and consumed', in other words offered by local unemployed individuals in certain neighbourhoods with a relatively high unemployment percentage.

But government control of employment can also be an obstacle for the supply of homeservices, like in some cases in Austria and Germany. In

Austria, trade licences are strictly regulated to narrowly-defined professions, which leads to the situation that, for instance, a potential one-man enterprise of a janitor offering caretaking services would need several licences, from a plumber's licence to that of an electrician. This applies also for other service providers, if they want to offer a bundle of services that are not closely related to each other. Also housing organizations face this problem, but those housing organizations that offer homeservices deal with it by creating a subsidiary for facility management that has the legal rights to perform certain services. Similarly in Germany many handicraft operations were previously reserved for trained master craftsmen. But recently changes in the German trade ordinance opened the homeservice market for unskilled workers. Furthermore in 2003, new regulations for the so-called 'mini-jobs' (with a wage up to 400 €) determined a fixed rate of depreciation applied for tax purposes as well as minor social security contributions. Both of these amended laws make it easier for unskilled workers to offer homeservices at a reasonable price.

In Germany, the so-called second job market, within which homeservices could create employment, is controlled by the government. The second job market is marked by a disproportionate share of unskilled workers. But employment services are the sole responsibility of the Federal Ministry of Economics and Labour and the respective municipal employment offices. Private recruitment agencies are restricted to the intermediation of temporary employment. Consequently, employment processes for subsidised jobs, such as those for the long-term unemployed, are often marked by bureaucratic obstacles and service providers have practically no possibility to choose the person for their needs. Moreover, those jobs are often short-term and extensions often result in a change of the employee.

Housing regulation

Housing market legislation influences the conditions for homeservice provision in many ways. We will not go into detail here, but give a couple of examples only. For instance, in many countries social housing organizations were earlier only mandated to provide affordable housing. In some countries like the Netherlands and Finland, the housing regulation has been liberalised considerably over the last decade, but despite this the Dutch Housing Act, for instance, still sets limitations on the business activities of social housing organizations. According to the Act, their business has to be in the field of social housing and they are not allowed to undertake activities that are not in the interest of social housing. This Act restricts the freedom of social housing organizations when it comes to developing new businesses, creating services and making profit. But since social housing organizations are nowadays allowed to set up subsidiaries, those interested usually offer homeservices in that way. In Spain the activities of housing managers are highly regulated, which leaves little room for additional initiatives.

To give another specific example of a regulatory restriction, in Germany the II Operating Cost Ordinance bans most costs for homeservices from being transferred to rents. In order for homeservices to be charged for in the rent, all tenants must agree to supplementary changes in their tenancy contracts. Moreover, housing organizations are not allowed to pass on to the tenants any investments in social infrastructure, such as concierge or common rooms. Both restrictions aggravate the financing of homeservices. There is, however, an exception: The German Energy Saving Act of 2003 determines strict regulations for energy-efficient building standards and thus permits housing organizations to transfer investments in energy-efficient building infrastructure to the rents.

MARKET FACTORS

In the beginning of this chapter it was contended that the prevalent culture of ownership as well as the imperative to possess material goods make it difficult for sustainable homeservices to penetrate to the market – even in such instances where they would be cost-efficient and make the lives of their users easier. Nevertheless there are trends that pave the way for home-services. In this section we will discuss those main trends as well as the factors that counteract them. These trends mainly concern homeservices in general, not sustainable homeservices specifically. They touch upon social sustainability, but they have no direct environmental sustainability implications. The environmental effects will depend upon how the services are designed.

Aging and changing lifestyles support homeservices

As the population is aging in all European countries and as an increase in institutional care is limited due to the lack of financial resources, there is a tendency to encourage elderly people to live at home as long as possible. This is also generally preferred by the elderly themselves. Independent living requires an increase in homeservices especially in the area of care and supervision. Services such as meals-on-wheels, security telephones, transportation and personal care services are relevant examples. Also new concepts like 'senior housing', that is housing for relatively fit seniors of the age 55 or more, are likely to gain ground as a form of housing (Ahlqvist, Heiskanen and Kallio 2005, for more service-intensive alternatives see also the Augustinum housing foundation in Jonuschat and Scharp 2004 and at www.sustainable-homeservices.com).

Due to lifestyle changes, there is on average less time than before available for domestic work, which contributes to increasing demand for certain homeservices. In addition to the elderly, families with children are the ones with a relatively high need to use homeservices (Varjonen et al. 2005). This is aggravated by the fact that both spouses of the family more often work even in Southern Europe or countries like in Austria, where such arrangements were uncommon until recently. Various types of home care service are needed by these families to alleviate the time pressures.

Throughout the Western countries the number of single households is growing and in the Central and Northern European cities studied, single households already amount to about 50 per cent of all households (Halme and Anttonen, 2004; Jasch et al, 2004; Jonuschat and Scharp, 2004; Kortman et al, 2004). In the southern cities of our sample the respective figure is still only around 20 per cent (Serrano and Velte, 2004; Trindade et al, 2004). Some of these single people are affluent individuals with lifestyles that do not favour household work and therefore they form a promising market segment for some homeservices.

To pick up a specific point that may facilitate the demand for homeservices, the internet can be applied in various ways for offering homeservices. Namely, it provides a new, relatively inexpensive marketing channel for homeservices. In addition to obvious issues such as homeservice providers' websites on the internet, there are other developments, such as the Finnish

Work Efficiency Institute's ELIAS service, an internet market place for homeservices. This virtual market place lists the services of over 400 providers, including a variety of homeservices such as cleaning, gardening, small repairs, food services, health care services, errand services, walking assistance, and other services like hairdressers and so on (see Chapter 2 for other features of ELIAS). In a survey it was found that an absolute majority of the providers experienced an increase in business due to this channel. Moreover, the internet can assist in the distribution process of homeservices. For instance, home delivery services of organic groceries nowadays mainly operate over the internet.

One of the most typical obstacles is that customers are not used to using homeservices, and hence there is a limited demand. This seems to be the case in Austria, Finland and the Netherlands. Especially in Finland and to some extent in Austria, this fact is due to the do-it-yourself mentality. In Finland it is typically considered that only elderly or disabled people, who can no longer take care of themselves, need services. Especially among the population over 50 years of age, using services is somewhat shameful because it symbolises a loss of the ability to cope independently with daily life (Varjonen et al. 2005). In Austria, the do-it-yourself attitude is closely linked to a culture of thriftiness. But in both countries this attitude is beginning to change among the younger population. Our resident surveys indicated that Spain and Portugal are quite different in this respect. According to the mentality of these countries it is good to use services and, contrary to Finland, the social impression of service use is positive: One can afford to use services and does not have to do everything oneself.

Costs

In the previous section costs were mentioned as one of the main obstacles to homeservice use. This may manifest itself in a reluctance to pay even if one could afford to do so. Yet on the other hand there are many people who cannot afford homeservices even if they would really need them. In other words, the cost of homeservices is partially a matter of attitude but to a degree also a real financial constraint. If we try to get a general overview of the question, a statistical comparison of the financial burden caused by the housing costs may give some indication of how much money households have available for extra homeservices. As regards the countries in our sample, the Dutch people are best off, only three per cent of the households encounter heavy financial burden due to housing costs, and 76 per cent are without any burden in this respect. Finland comes after the Netherlands, with 11 per cent of households experiencing a heavy burden, and 56 per cent facing no burden at all. In Spain and Portugal housing costs form a heavy burden for approximately one-fourth of the households, and only 16.5 per cent of the Spanish and 25 per cent of the Portuguese households do not experience a burden due to housing costs. Austria and Germany lie in between these two groups (Eurostat, 2004, and Table 7 in Chapter 3).

If one would draw a conclusion – albeit a somewhat mechanistic one – from the above figures, it would be that of the countries in this sample, the Dutch homeservice providers have the best possibilities to find customers that can afford to pay homeservices. In this sense Spain is the sample country worst off. Costs are a great problem in the provision of social services to households. Families are simply not able to shoulder the burden of private care at home, so that there is a high risk that these jobs are taken over by immigrants who cannot obtain working permits and thus have to accept very low wages. As mentioned above, another matter is naturally the willingness to pay. According to the cultural norms in Spain and Portugal people would on average be willing to pay for homeservices, but their finances are limited. In the Northern and Central European countries of the sample, on average, the actual ability to pay for homeservices is higher, but the cultural norm or general attitude favours saving money on these kinds of expenses (see also Chapter 3).

Particularly ecologically-oriented homeservices like those oriented toward energy and water savings can reduce the housing costs of the residents. Sometimes also waste management services, for instance counselling on waste reduction or separation, can reduce costs. High energy and water prices add to the attraction of such services, both for housing organizations and the residents. For instance, in Germany operating and resource costs have continuously risen during the last years, and hence customer demands for counselling on reducing housing costs have increased. Expenditures on housing, water, electricity, gas and other fuels consumption are highest in Finland and Germany, amounting to approximately 25 per cent of the total household expenditure. In Austria and the Netherlands they form around 20 per cent of total household expenditure, whereas in Portugal and Spain they only make up 10 and 14 per cent of total household spending (Eurostat, 2004). On the other hand, the relative share of electricity, gas and other fuels consumption of household consumption is the smallest in Finland (2 per cent), Spain (2.2 per cent) and Portugal (2.6 per cent), whereas in the other three sample countries the share is clearly higher, between 3.4 and 3.9 per cent (Eurostat, 2004 and Table 8 in Chapter 3).

These figures appear to correlate rather well with the popularity of homeservices directed toward energy and water savings in these countries. They are common and popular in all four countries where expenditure on both of these categories is relatively high. These services do not seem to exist at all in Spain and Portugal, where expenditure on both categories is low. We do not, however, argue that this is the sole reason behind the popularity of resource saving homeservices. We assume that the general attitude toward environmental protection in the country is an intervening factor.

In addition to utility costs (in relation to income or total household expenditure), the form of collecting utility fees has an impact on the attractiveness of resource-saving services. If these fees are collected as a lump sum, there is less willingness among the residents to use these services, because they do not directly see the savings. In Austria the common practice is to charge energy costs from individual households per consumption, but water is usually charged in a lump sum. Occasionally also warm water is charged separately. In Finland and Germany electricity and heating are charged according to consumption, but a lump sum is the common form charging for water except for new buildings, where separate billing of water usage is becoming a norm. In general, in Spain and Portugal there are separate meters for cold water and electricity, meaning that they are paid for according to consumption. In the Netherlands electricity, heating gas and water are normally charged according to consumption, expect for Amsterdam were water is charged with a standard monthly tariff. One of the effective ways of encouraging resource savings would be to move to individual billing of electricity, heating and water.

However, there is evidence that even when households are not charged individually, a motivation for savings can be created. Cost savings can be used to reduce rents, or to avoid raising the rents. Alternatively they can be spent for some common good purpose like organizing house parties, acquiring new equipment for the building or the like (Halme and Anttonen, 2004).

As to the costs of additional homeservices such as laundry service, apartment cleaning and the like that could be offered or mediated by the housing organization, the charging method needs to be appropriate and furthermore it needs to communicated clearly. In an Austrian survey it appeared that residents often had of the wrong impression about the charging method for extra homeservices (Hrauda et al, 2002). Some residents are afraid of ending up paying for services that they neither want to have nor make use of. This breeds reluctance toward homeservice provision in general. Whenever feasible, the best solution may be to charge extra services per unit consumed and moreover communicate the cost basis well.

PRACTICES AND NORMS OF THE HOUSING INDUSTRY

There are some practices, norms and taken-for-granted ways of doing things within the housing industry and among the related service providers that influence homeservice provision. These norms and practices are naturally intertwined with and influenced by legislative changes, or market/customer pressure. Nevertheless they warrant a separate discussion because norms and culture steer decision-making, choices and action more subtly and indirectly than legislation or market pressure.

Housing or service providers?

Some innovative housing organizations – both private and social ones – show signs of an emerging service mentality. Their role is changing from building care-takers toward providers of 'living arrangements'. As regards social housing organizations in Austria, Finland, Germany and the Netherlands, this is at least partially a result of profit-orientation following from changes in the legal status of these organizations. Housing organizations have perceived that homeservices enable them to improve the loyalty of the tenants and thereby reduce negligence and vandalism as well as get longer tenancies. For some Austrian and Finnish social housing organizations, an incentive for the supply of homeservices is the fact that the value of the dwelling or building block rises. Their competitive position improves and thus higher prices and rents can be obtained. However, despite these developments many housing organizations still consider mere housing provision as their core business and concentrate on it, thus disregarding homeservice ideas.

Cooperation in service provision

As changes in housing regulation have brought about the disappearance of care-takers, janitors or 'las porteras' who used to live on the premises they have also resulted in a re-organizing of the traditional homeservice setting. In Finland and the Netherlands these changes started a decade ago, whereas in Austria and Spain they are more current. In the former countries this change has meant increasing cooperation between housing organizations and other service providers. In one sense this cooperation can facilitate the emergence of homeservices. In Finland housing organizations have outsourced many activities traditionally considered to belong to them, such as all maintenance duties. As large maintenance firms have recently started to also offer other than maintenance services, for instance various care services, this makes it possible for them to extend their homeservice offerings and include personal home care concepts into their service palette. The benefit from the customer's perspective is that multiple services are available via one provider. In the Netherlands some large housing organizations are establishing subsidiaries for this same purpose. In Portugal the management of apartment buildings is either taken care of by the residents themselves or entrusted to a professional housing manager or condominium management company. For competitive reasons, condominium management companies tend to offer a broader selection of homeservices by co-operating with service companies. The market for this kind of services is increasing, especially in upper class neighbourhoods.

On the other hand the disappearance of the janitor culture has signified a loss of informal help, in other words informal service offerings at home. Besides, commercially produced homeservices and the cooperation of housing organizations with commercial service firms are not the only option for providing homeservices. Indeed, it may be that in some instances the increased   profit-orientation   and   business-mindedness   of   housing organizations does not necessarily mean an increase or improvement in homeservice provision, at least not for all residents. Unlike in the other focal countries, German social housing organizations are used to working with non-profit organizations to alleviate social problems by homeservice provision. Housing organizations can utilise the knowledge and capability resources of NPOs. These partnerships enhance the provision of especially socially sustainable homeservices. The pressure to privatise social housing is a threat to the provision of socially-oriented homeservices, because underprivileged market segments are usually not of interest for commercial providers. These groups still call for the attention of the non-profit service providers.

Despite the emergence of partnerships and cooperation, there is still strong sectoral thinking to be observed at least in Finland and the Netherlands. For instance, housing organizations and public social and health services do not seem to easily find ways to work together. However, as public spending is being cut, the public sector is increasingly procuring its mandatory services from non-profit organizations. They are likely to be more flexible in service provision and can also more easily offer extra homeservices, provided financing can be arranged.

Occasionally, rapid liberalization and an over-emphasis on cost-orientation can lead to unintended consequences. Since the mid-1990s, almost all real estate maintenance services in Finland have been outsourced to maintenance companies. At that time the real estate maintenance business was released from any requirements that were considered to hinder competition. Anybody was allowed to set up a maintenance company. This has lead to an abundance of these firms, and to subsequent fierce competition in which the dominant competitive factor is price. As a result, maintenance firms are caught up in 'a race for the bottom', offering minimal services as cheaply as possible. Maintenance firms would be a natural actor to offer other services than only the minimal 'snow shovelling & sanding', but it can be argued that except for the few large ones, there are many small companies that lack the skills, service mentality, and monetary incentive to extend their service offering. According to the interviews of Finnish housing sectors experts, the maintenance profession is still not well educated and the companies in general do not tend to be very innovative.

PHYSICAL INFRASTRUCTURE

Building infrastructure and city design have an indirect but substantial role with regard to homeservice supply. One of the many questions is that the provision of some services requires space in the building or on the premises. When building land is expensive there is a tendency to save on costs by using all possible space for dwellings, instead of leaving common space in the building. When housing organizations have buildings constructed or individual apartment buyers make investment decisions, they first and foremost try to minimize the up-front cost. As every square meter of common space increases the price, common spaces are created only in buildings where it is required by the city plan. There are some exceptions like for instance high-income neighbourhoods in Portugal, where common spaces like saunas, swimming pools, or roof-top patios make the building more attractive for wealthy buyers.

Sometimes the need for common space is a broader issue concerning the relation between space in the building and the premises, and on the level of the entire neighbourhood. For instance in cities or towns where there are only a few public playgrounds or they are uncomfortable or unsafe, a playground in the building yard may improve the residents' quality of life such as social contacts between mothers and children. On the other hand in cities like Helsinki, where the density of public playgrounds is high and they are well-equipped and enhanced by social activities offered by the playground personnel, the importance of a playground on the premises is not that relevant for the residents.

Apart from that, all over Europe the urban planning paradigm of functional separation of the 1960s and 1970s led to the design of mono-functional living districts in the outskirts. The so-called 'sleeping towns' are marked by strong deficiencies in commercial infrastructure. Thus the role of city planners is crucial in indirectly facilitating the homeservice supply.

PROMOTING SUSTAINABLE HOUSEHOLD SERVICES

Why have services as a route toward more sustainable household consumption not spread faster and wider even in instances where they would increase the users' quality of life? Among other things, infrastructures and cultural mentalities favouring the ownership of goods, on the top of incorrect market incentives, are factors that slow down the penetration of sustainable services as forms of consumption. These factors can be changed or circumvented. It takes an effort from the change agents and often requires cooperation between several actors representing different sectors of society, but it is possible. There are also incentives and trends that support a service orientation, which service promoters can utilise. In this section we discuss the ways to remove the main obstacles and to utilise the supportive trends.

Potential markets for household services are offered by trends such as the aging population that needs services to continue living at home, time constraints of working families and a segment of single people wishing to outsource some of their domestic tasks. From the supply perspective, developments in ICTs have made it possible to offer some services at a lower cost. This potential is, however, counteracted by lack of information about homeservices among the potential users and, secondly, the fact that those in need of services are often not used to using them, or cannot afford them. To reach these potential customers, different strategies are called for. For customers who could afford to pay for services, but for attitudinal reasons do not use them, strategies aiming at attitude change are necessary. Attitudes can be changed to some degree by making homeservices available so easily that pioneering customers start to use them, setting a model for others to follow. This is likely to pave the way for more service-based consumption patterns. On the other hand, for those who are in need of homeservices, but cannot afford them, strategies should primarily aim at finding suitable financing structures. In many instances, cooperation of the public sector and NPOs or social enterprises may offer feasible solutions.

As to designing actual services in practice, it should be kept in mind that for different national contexts, different strategies are required, as mentioned in Chapter 3. One of these differences is that different promotion strategies are called for in 'do-it-yourself' countries, versus 'service-favouring' countries. In do-it-yourself cultures, introducing relatively new sustainable homeservices and mediating their use would be a potential approach. A component of the user's own participation could also be crafted into the service in order to reduce the costs and the mental barrier to use services. However, in countries where consumers already use services, a more viable general approach could be to improve the sustainability of already existing services.

Likewise, there are also numerous national differences regarding practices and norms in the housing industry that influence homeservice provision. Irrespectively of this, however, housing organizations and other similar actors – such as housing management companies, building promoters, or maintenance companies – could assist considerably in the provision of services to households in ways that enhance sustainability. These actors can be service providers or intermediaries, depending on the incentives related to their market position.

The trend of liberalization of the housing market and legislation, and the subsequent business orientation of housing organizations may support these pursuits, although this trend can also have negative implications from the homeservice perspective. On the positive side the liberalization means more flexibility in operations and an incentive to develop a service mentality. A similarity across the four northern countries of the sample was that some housing organizations are beginning to see homeservice provision as a business opportunity because of the indirect customer loyalty and image effects. This can be best observed in Finland and the Netherlands, where both the social housing market as well as parts of the related homeservice market were liberalised in the mid-1990s. This has led to an increased business orientation of the field, which is shaping the homeservice supply. In Austria and to some extent Germany a similar trend is starting now. This opens up possibilities for different types of co-operative arrangements, as housing organizations do not tend to provide new services with their own personnel, but seek for collaborators.

However, the dynamic of obstacles and incentives differs between countries depending on whether there are large (often at least formerly social) housing organizations or whether private ownership of dwellings is the predominant form of housing. In the latter case housing organizations cannot be a major agent with regard to homeservice provision or mediation, but other facilitating actors and structures must be considered. In these situations condominium associations, and particularly housing management companies and other service providers like maintenance companies become relevant. If these actors do not show spontaneous interest toward homeservices, SMEs, larger companies or NPOs that want to offer services can take the lead by initiating collaboration. Organizations that have an immediate connection to households via the building are a good channel for marketing services to households.

The cost of household services was experienced as a hindrance in all the studied countries. Occasionally this hindrance is psychological and manifests itself in that people do not want to pay for outsourcing tasks, that they could basically do themselves. Nevertheless, for some the cost restriction is real. Due to the high costs, part of homeservice provision is transferred to the black market. From the perspective of developing innovative homeservices in general, and sustainable homeservices in particular, this is a negative issue. In Austria, Finland and Germany indirect labour costs were pointed out as one reason for the high cost of services. In these instances there was some positive evidence that a tax deduction opportunity for households acquiring homeservice, as well as regulative concessions regarding low-paid service jobs, increase the use of homeservices. To address the cost barrier not only nationally but in the European context also some EU level actions could be taken, such as reducing the indirect labour costs of low-paid service jobs.

Secondly, it would be advisable to increase the support of social enterprises, because they could play a considerably larger role in homeservice provision. They are an excellent vehicle for offering novel services – especially labour-intensive ones that do not require high technological skills – that are considered too risky by commercial enterprises as long as they are unknown in the market. For instance many car-sharing companies have grown out of social enterprises, but today when the service model is more developed and known in the market, it is a profitable business for commercial enterprises, too. From the sustainability perspective, social enterprises can be expected to offer more environmentally conscious services. As to social sustainability, they offer employment to people who would not otherwise be able to enter the job market. From the perspective of the employees, the self-esteem gained is an invaluable advantage and, on the other hand society may indirectly benefit through improved social stability. This is also economi-cally beneficial because society saves money by not having to support unemployment. Instead, it gains employment opportunities and the ensuing benefits with lesser financial support.

Thirdly, as one of the major problems is the potential customers' lack of information about homeservices and their providers, national bodies interested in promoting service business, or the EU via its relevant structures could actively support actors (intermediaries) that mediate services from several small providers (for examples see ELIAS electronic market place for homeservices in www.sustainable-homeservices.com and Buenos Dias, Buenas Noches in www.buenosdiasbuenasnoches.com). This would offer a marketing channel to small service providers who seldom have financial possibilities to advertise their services, and on the other hand make it easy for citizens to get information about homeservices. The resulting increase in service use would mean more jobs in the service sector. These intermediary models could also involve features that encourage environmentally benign services, such as renovation with ecological materials, cleaning with environmentally benign detergents, ecological gardening and so on.

To summarise, there are a number of cultural and structural matters that influence the homeservice preferences and service framework, making it complicated to give general recommendations or to copy services as such from one national setting to another. The recommendations and services should always be designed for the conditions of the local service use culture and framework. Furthermore, the sustainability of services must still be carefully designed. Services in general or homeservices in particular do not automatically promote sustainability.

6 Business models and service development

Despite the abundance of innovation and ideas since the introduction of eco-efficient service thinking in the mid-1990s, only few truly eco-efficient or sustainable services have made their way to the market place. One of the reasons is the slow rate of change in institutions and cognitive structures. But there is also a lack of systematic analysis of the business perspective. Until sustainable service innovations are turned into concepts that are feasible in the market, the numerous instances for reducing resource consumption will remain nothing but unattainable ideals. In order to start fulfilling the knowledge gap about the business feasibility of sustainable services, this chapter asks what we can learn from both successful and incomplete elements of the business models of currently operational sustainable household services.

The latter section of the chapter introduces more detailed instructions for developing sustainable homeservices. The method is based on service engineering. 'Sustainable service engineering', as it is called here, is applicable not only for creating new services, but also for making existing services more sustainable. The method is relatively simple, but systematic, and it can be utilised by many types of service providers from business enterprises to non-profit and housing organizations.

BUSINESS MODELS OF SUSTAINABLE SERVICES

In recent years the term 'business model' has proliferated in the eco-efficient or sustainable service discussion. This is because it was widely recognised that one of the reasons for the failure of seemingly good eco-service concepts was the inadequate attention paid to the market viability of such services, especially in the case of consumer services. Even though the business model terminology has recently made its way into the discussions and writings of sustainable service promoters and researchers, it has mainly been used without any explanation of what is meant by it (Tukker and van Halen, 2003), or comprehended as mere revenue model (Vercalsteren and Gerken, 2004) or in terms of flowcharts portraying 'service logistics' (Tempelman, 2004). This is not surprising, because there is no established or comprehensive definition of the term 'business model' (Timmers 1999). Here we apply a framework that has its roots in the work of, for instance, Normann and Ramirez (1994) and Räsänen (2001). It is a simple model, yet it captures most of the relevant aspects that influence the viability of a service concept in the market. This business model framework allows us to scrutinize the competitive advantage of the services, the customer benefits, as well as the resources and capabilities of the providers of the service, and the financing arrangement. Hence we propose the following questions for probing the market viability of a service.

- What kinds of competitive advantage pertain to the sustainable service,
- Which benefits can users or customers derive from the service (in comparison to more traditional ways and means of fulfilling their needs)
- Which capabilities and other resources does the provider or the network of providers have, and
- How is the service financed?

The term business model is perhaps slightly misleading, because it at least implicitly refers to only commercially provided services. Yet the model is applicable for a service of any provider, be it an NGO, a public sector provider, a business enterprise or a network of these actors. One only needs to understand the elements of the business model framework in a flexible manner. It should be mentioned that this framework does not take a stand on the environmental effects of the service. Social effects are also captured only in a narrow sense in terms of user benefit. Consequently, in order to assess the sustainability aspects properly, this analytical model should be applied together with the sustainability evaluation tool introduced in Chapter 2. Incorporation of sustainability aspects into service design is also addressed in the latter part of this chapter.

Next some good practice sustainable service examples will be examined with the help of this framework. Since most of these services have been described in Chapter 2, only a short description is provided here, and the space is devoted to the business model analysis. The described services represent the following clusters: repair services, energy services and 'many services from same counter'. Since the delivery services of organic food and the cluster of 'eco-feature services' are fairly simple variations of an ordinary service concept, the basic business model of these service groups will be outlined only roughly. Furthermore, 'wide-range environmental counselling' services of Die Grüne Liga and Die Umweltberatung and are not described here. Instead, an interesting new development, the NU sustainable card scheme, is presented although strictly speaking it does not represent a homeservice but is rather another type of service that aims to promote more sustainable ways of consumption.

Business model of R.U.S.Z.'s repair and recycling service

R.U.S.Z. is a non-profit organization that repairs or dismantles and disposes of a wide range of household appliances. These appliances are gathered either from waste collection sites, picked up from offices or households, or delivered by individuals. Usable parts from irreparable appliances are collected for repairing other appliances. R.U.S.Z also sells repaired appliances and gives them a one-year warranty.

Competitive advantage for R.U.S.Z. originates from the organization's mission to repair and recycle used household appliances. It is a non-profit enterprise with a societal mission of making use of a problematic waste fragment: household appliances. Therefore there are parties that are interested in supporting R.U.S.Z. Moreover, the organization does not face fierce competition, because many equivalent commercial enterprises have withdrawn from the market. Part of its competitive advantage relates to the fact that R.U.S.Z is a social enterprise and it employs long-term unemployed or immigrants. Thus it gets support for their salaries and therefore the repair activity becomes feasible. In terms of customer base for repaired appliances, R.U.S.Z has a distinct target segment: low-income people who cannot afford new appliances. The warranty is an advantage in the competition with commercial enterprises, because they usually do not offer such long guarantee terms for used appliances.

Customer benefit. R.U.S.Z sells repaired appliances at affordable prices and gives them a one-year guarantee. Thus it helps low-income households to save money and provides the customers with the security that the second-hand appliance will be repaired or refunded if it breaks down. The latter point is actually one of the key questions for re-marketing used household appliances. If compared with the customers' other options for fulfilling their needs, those with very limited financial resources would either have to do without a certain appliance (TV, fridge or the like) or resort to the cheapest new appliances, thus also exposing themselves to low quality products that have a short lifetime. On the other hand, if we look at downstream customers, they benefit from getting rid of appliances that they no longer can make use of.

Capabilities and resources. R.U.S.Z trains long-term unemployed and other disadvantaged people to collect, repair and dismantle electrical and electronic household appliances. Thus the organization possesses the capabilities to train unskilled labour. The work force of R.U.S.Z is well motivated, because the work opportunity gives the employees feelings of self-esteem and participation in society, which many of them have been lacking for a long period of time. R.U.S.Z also passes on the repairing skills outside the enterprise itself, because the technical and social skills of the R.U.S.Z employees enable them to enter the normal labour market, which is one of goals of R.U.S.Z. On the other hand, R.U.S.Z has the collection network for used appliances, in other words contacts to waste collection authorities and sites, and to some enterprises that recycle their used appliances via R.U.S.Z.

Financing of the service. R.U.S.Z is partially funded by the City of Vienna, and the investment of the city is planned to pay off in three years. Furthermore, the City of Vienna avoids paying unemployment allowances, because R.U.S.Z employs previously unemployed people. It also saves in waste handling costs. Part of the funding of R.U.S.Z comes from the sales of repaired appliances and maintenance service that it offers to other organizations. Furthermore, R.U.S.Z organizes repair courses at some Viennese evening schools. However, when the WEEE directive (directive on waste electronic and electrical equipment that makes producers, importers and sellers of electronic and electrical appliances responsible for take-back of their products) becomes fully enforced, R.U.S.Z has a prospect to become economically self-sufficient. However, enterprises like R.U.S.Z cannot be the solution for managing waste from all electronic and electrical appliances, and thus large industrial recycling systems are bound to be established. Due to the social benefits and the innovation basis residing in plural systems, smaller scale reuse and recycling enterprises should be encouraged to co-exist alongside large industrial recyclers.

Business model of Motiva's resident as energy expert service

In terms of competitive advantage, energy saving services are perhaps best compared with other possible forms of organizing such services or with other ways of promoting energy saving in households. The 'Resident as energy expert' is a concept that involves voluntary experts who monitor the building's energy and water consumption and advise other residents on energy saving, the housing organization and housing management that provide the energy and water consumption data, and Motiva, the Finnish Energy Efficiency Centre which trains the experts and promotes the concept (see Chapter 2).

The *competitive advantage* of the 'Resident as energy expert' service is that it involves residents in advising others on energy and water savings and is thus a peer model rather than an authoritative top-down approach. This is likely to create motivation and commitment among service users, because the 'expert' is one of 'us' – easy to approach – rather than a remote specialist. Furthermore, the service makes use of the enthusiasm of willing volunteers.

It should, however, be noted that the above depends on the character of the expert. It has been observed that the more socially skilful the expert is, the more interested the residents of the building are in the service.

Customer benefits of any energy saving service are cost reductions and improved living conditions such as the right temperature in the dwelling. Moreover it offers a more direct channel to housing management. Compared to other energy savings services described in Chapter 2, the energy expert model does not demand any investments from the user unlike, for instance, the EPA-concept.

As to *capabilities and resources* of the providers of this service, there are three partners that provide the service in cooperation. The Centre for Energy Efficiency, Motiva, is responsible for training the experts. It has a large network of trainers that instruct voluntary residents on energy expert courses. Motiva also maintains extranet services for energy experts in order to keep their level of knowledge up-to-date. Housing organizations and housing managers, on the other hand, have access to energy and water consumption data, which they make available for the energy expert.

As to *financing*, due to the volunteer work the service is produced with little cost. Training and the measurement device kit of an energy expert cost 80 euros, which is usually paid by the housing organization. It is a minor investment when compared with the savings that accrue.

Business model of ELIAS internet market place of homeservices

ELIAS is an internet market place for more than 400 homeservices from eight service sectors spanning from care and cleaning to renovation and gardening. The service was launched in 2000 by the Finnish Work Efficiency Institute (TTS) (see Chapter 2).

The competitive advantage of ELIAS is that it combines many services within the same website and is the only one of its kind in Finland. Elements that support homeservice use, such as instructions for contracts between households and service providers or for making tax deductions, also add to the popularity of this virtual market. From the providers perspective, ELIAS is a free marketing channel with which it is possible to reach several potential customers.

Customers benefit from ELIAS firstly because they can find information about homeservice providers in one place and do not have to conduct time-consuming internet or other searches. Secondly, ELIAS guarantees a certain level of reliability of the provider, because the TTS screens that service providers listed in ELIAS making sure they are registered companies. It also gains feedback from customers and if it turns out that a service provider does not deliver services as promised, the provider may be removed from ELIAS. Furthermore, service providers in ELIAS have a quality ranking of providers, which users can utilize when choosing a provider. The quality ranking also indicates whether the provider has participated in TTS' training which includes the eco-efficiency of service provision.

Capabilities and resources. The Work Efficiency Institute has the mandate to serve households and enterprises among others, by proving education, research and information services. ELIAS fits well within the umbrella of TTS' activities. ELIAS is a result, on one hand, of the enthusiasm of one of TTS' employees with a long-term research background on organizing homeservices in various countries, and on the other hand, of the network and mandate of TTS which have given it the credibility to organize the virtual market place.

Financing. During the first years the service is partially funded by EU and the regional government of Southern Finland, which wants to promote employment in the service industry. The experiences are mainly positive. Small service providers consider that they have found more customers with the help of the internet market place. Use of homeservices has increased in Finland, and in the southern areas of the country, ELIAS is considered one of the facilitators of this trend. In general TTS finances its activities by sales of educational services, R&D services, publications, membership fees and partially governmental funding. It is foreseen that entrepreneurs listed in ELIAS could pay a fee since the service is a relatively inexpensive way to market their services. On the other hand, the regional government is interested in enhancing jobs within the service industry and sees ELIAS as a means for that end, and may thus support ELIAS financially in the future as well.

Business model of NU-Spaarpas, the sustainable incentive card scheme

NU-Spaarpas, the sustainable incentive card scheme in Rotterdam, encourages people to consume more sustainably by rewarding them for choosing goods and services that meet the sustainability criteria. 'Sustainable' in this case refers to both environmental and social sustainability. Among other things, purchasing fair trade or eco-labelled or second-hand products, having items repaired, or borrowing or renting (art, tools) qualify as sustainable consumption. Started in 2002, the card is now accepted in 100 shops and municipal services in Rotterdam. There are some 10,000 cardholders. Every cardholder buying a sustainable product or service from a shop or other organization that participates in the NU scheme receives NU points. These points are automatically credited to their chip cards. For each euro spent, the consumer receives a number of NU points that can be spent in participating shops or other organizations (van Sambeek and Kampers, 2004).

Competitive advantage. The NU card scheme rewards consumers for sustainable consumption decisions rather than 'punishing' for them in form of higher prices. Consumers can make savings by buying sustainably. The NU card is valid in many shops and among service providers. It is an affordable marketing tool for SMEs to attract and retain customers. It makes use of the 'card and savings' trend.

Customer benefit. The NU scheme offers savings for sustainable purchases or sustainable behaviour like waste separation and makes it easier to find information about sustainable products and services.

Capabilities and resources. The core group of the NU scheme involves the Rotterdam transport authority, Roteb sanitation department, Rabobank Rotterdam, and Stichting Points. In the larger network there are, for instance, more than 100 shops, museums of Rotterdam, and many other municipal service institutions.

Financing. The launch stage of the NU scheme is co-funded by the European Commission, the Province of South Holland and the Ministry of Housing, Spatial Planning and the Environment. As to the cardholders, they receive points when buying sustainable products or services. For each euro spent the consumer receives a set number of NU points, which can be used as if they had monetary value. Cardholders can redeem the points at participating shops or other service providing organizations. Rewards include, among other things, day passes for public transportation, admissions to local attractions and museums. Points can also be exchanged for 'green specials' at participating shops. The parties granting points pay the NU card scheme 0.7 euro cents per point, plus a nominal fee for administration costs. The points that savers redeem are refunded to the receiving businesses by the NU card scheme at their trade value: 0.7 euro cents per point.

Business models of ordinary services with eco-features

In Chapter 2 we described quite a few homeservices, such as home delivery of organic food and groceries, eco-gardening or the mobile cook preparing food with organic ingredients, which are variations of commonplace services such as home delivery or gardening. With regard to their business models, characteristic to these services is that the ecological feature forms the competitive advantage of the service, because they cater for the so-called 'ecologically active' consumers who are willing to pay more for ecological features of their products and services. The capabilities of the providers stem from the fact that they have skills in the respective service area (gardening), but also knowledge about ecological products (such as natural fertilizers). Both of these, as well as ability to design the other elements of the service sufficiently in accord with the principles of sustainable development, are needed in order to provide the service.

COMMONALITIES OF SUCCESSFUL HOMESERVICE BUSINESS MODELS

The business model framework introduced above can also be used as a starting point when planning new services or developing existing ones. When thinking about the illustrated business models or the larger set of services studied for this book, a number of questions arise. Are there any commonalities in the business of the sustainable household service examples studied? What can be learnt from the successful elements of these services? What are the most typical deficiencies in these service concepts and how to improve them?

As regards the competitive advantage and customer benefit dimensions of business models, they pertain very much to individual services, and it is not meaningful to generalize much between the different services. However, regarding the capabilities and resources of the providers as well as financing arrangements, it is possible to draw some notions worth discussing.

Networks

In many instances the creation of a successful service requires the involvement of multiple actors across sectors (Mont, 2004). The above services like 'resident as energy expert' (and a number of other energy saving services), the R.U.S.Z repair and recycling service and the 'virtual market place for homeservices' all involve a network of actors rather than one single provider. Especially successful energy efficiency services seem to benefit from the involvement of the housing organization. Some of the energy service concepts are outright impossible to implement without help from the housing organization. NU-Spaarpas, the sustainable incentive card scheme in Rotterdam is based on cross-sectoral networks of multiple actors. Beyond the evidence in this book, the car-sharing organizations with the best market penetration, like Mobility in Switzerland or StattAuto in Berlin, co-operate with municipal transport authorities, bus companies and railways.

The 'ordinary service with eco-features' cluster, on the other hand, is different. The success of services in this cluster often appears to depend on their providers' capability to offer a good-quality service and find a clientele that is interested in paying a premium for an eco-feature of the service.

Public sector facilitation

One the commonalities for the services studied here is that relatively often a public sector actor facilitates service provision, at least when the service is being launched. The most typical form of facilitation is financing the initiation of a service. This is not a trendy observation at times when a tendency to operate on a pure business basis dominates. However, many present institutions and infrastructures tend to favour material consumption, and thus in order to introduce new ways of fulfilling needs and living everyday lives, some kind public facilitation is often necessary. One could even argue that one condition of service success in quite a few instances is the cooperation of sustainable service providers and promoters with relevant public sector actors.

The involvement of the public sector can vary from mere financing to other forms of input like providing parking places for car-sharing cars or the like. Furthermore, public provision is perhaps the best way to organize some services. For example – beyond the discussion about 'consumer services offered directly at home' – warm school lunches or public libraries are typical concepts in the Nordic countries. These services are both eco-efficient and socially sustainable, although seldom considered as examples of 'sustainable services'.

Having said that, however, we also acknowledge that a disproportionate share of the services studied here depend on public financing. This is partially due to an early stage of the development of the field. In the longer term, when sustainable services become a more accepted and common part of consumption, the direction should be toward financially independent service concepts. However, also in a long-term perspective some services may be best organized in public-private cooperation. This goes especially for cases in which the economic profitability of the whole system benefits from that cooperation. To give one example, support of social enterprises may at first glance appear as merely a form of welfare aid. However, if scrutinizing the macro-economic effects, society saves in unemployment benefits and gets productive labour in return.

One of the most sensible roles of a public actor is perhaps to assist citizens in finding services. Often providers and potential users needing services do not meet due to information asymmetry. The diffusion of information and communication technologies like the internet give public actors new relatively inexpensive means for creating facilitating concepts such as 'service data banks' or the like.

ICT is a good servant

A fair number of the good-practice homeservices made use of relatively common ICTs such as the internet or mobile phones. E-commerce concepts of organic food or groceries are typical examples. Marketing homeservices on the internet is yet another example. The car-sharing service of CityCarClub in Finland and Sweden operates the car door locks with mobile phones and thus removes the hassle of key exchange.

Futuristic ICT-based services or product-services, such as remote control of homes or 'fridges that think for you' (communicate with the mobile phones of users), have not appeared successful in the market at least yet, except for special need areas. One of the exceptions is health monitoring of elderly, where remote monitoring with wrist devices that are in 24-h connection to chosen recipient are relatively successful (see VIVAGO in Chapter 2 and www.sustainable-homeservices.com). A key point, however, is not to start service design from the technology perspective. Customer needs or user benefits should be the point of departure.

The general business model framework exemplifies issues that should be taken into account when evaluating the feasibility of a service concept. In the next section we will introduce a procedure for service engineering, which is a more detailed way into service development.

SERVICE ENGINEERING: IMPROVING THE SUSTAINABILITY PROFILE OF SERVICES

The method called 'sustainable service engineering' is not only applicable for creating new services, but can also be applied for making existing services more sustainable. The method is relatively simple, but systematic. We acknowledge that in reality service providing organizations seldom create services in such a systematic fashion. Services often come about in a more haphazard fashion, by copying from others, from flash ideas, or by random stepwise development, which is not guided by any systematic master plan of service engineering. These ways are probably just as good most of the time, yet we find that many service providers could make use of the method presented here, or at least parts of it may provide new input for the service development work. According to one of the main messages of this book, we pay special attention to housing organizations as homeservice providers, but the method introduced is equally applicable also for other service providers, as will be shown.

Because of the origin of the method, the term 'service engineering' is used instead of speaking about 'service design', for instance, which would be more in line with the terminology applied in the product-service-systems or eco-efficient service community, or the Anglo-American scientific service developers' community. In this chapter service engineering will be used in a broad sense referring to the whole process of the systematic development of services. The first traces of the concept can be found in the Anglo-American discussion on 'new service development' in the 1970s and 1980s (Bowers, 1985). The term service engineering, referring to systematic service development using relevant instruments, methods and tools, was coined more recently (Ramaswamy, 1996; Mandelbaum, 1999). Mandelbaum defined the goal of service engineering as follows: 'The goal of service engineering is to develop scientifically-based design principles and tools (often culminating in software), that support and balance service quality and efficiency, from the likely conflicting perspectives of customers, service providers, managers and society'. Service engineering as a concept could be used in different ways, for instance as mentioned above for developing new services as well as for the redesign of existing services. Like the different approaches of product engineering, the framework of service engineering is open to different development goals.

There are several linear, circular or loop-based models, which could be used as a framework to guide the service development team (cf. DIN, 1998). In practice the choice of any of these models is not crucial, because time and personnel capacity set their own limitations on the service engineering team. Nevertheless every model is connected to somewhat different methods for creating, designing, implementing or evaluating services. Due to the breadth of methods for the generation of new ideas (such as brainstorming or brain writing) or for the participation of potential customers or users (e.g. focus groups or the lead user method), it is not easy to outline a concept of service engineering suitable for different branches, like the housing sector or municipal or commercial service providers, as well as for different types of services. Two of the important problems here are problems of rating (see Chapter 2) and the involvement of customers. Nevertheless, a recent study shows that these and some other problems may be solved in a relatively satisfactory manner. In that study a guideline for service engineering was developed, which on the one hand guides the service development team, but on the other hand leaves sufficient freedom for modifying or adapting the systems on the basis of the special conditions of the services or goals (Hohm et al, 2004).

The model developed by Hohm et al. (2004) is applied here for developing sustainable homeservices. This linear model includes four steps: situation analysis, service creation, service design and service management. Within each step one can distinguish between a sub-phase of development (except the situation analysis, which starts as an analysis) and a rating or evaluation of the results of the development sub-phase (Figure 9).

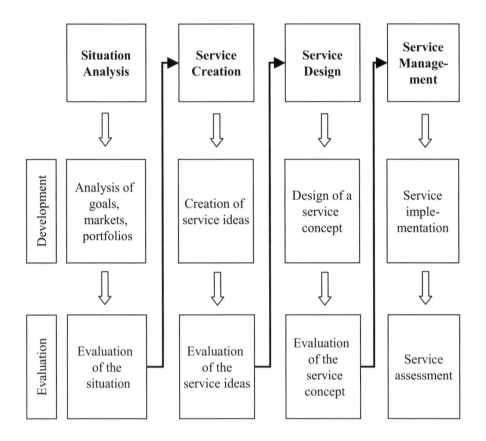

Figure 9. *Main service engineering phaces*

Many providers offering homeservices that can potentially enhance sustainable development are not solely in 'the sustainability business'. Housing organizations, and many commercial service providers as well as the municipal ones, face many other service determinants apart from sustainability – sometimes they may even be quite unaware of sustainability concerns. Consequently in this chapter we start by describing the different steps of model first without referring to sustainability. Afterwards the special conditions of sustainable service engineering are explained for every step. Furthermore we try to exemplify that the model is flexible enough to be adapted for different organizations and their corresponding service portfolios.

Step 1: Situation Analysis

The situation analysis aims to detect and specify goals for the service engineering process as well as to explore the relevant framework conditions that could obstruct or support an implementation of homeservices in the market. It can be divided into an analysis of goals, market conditions and the homeservice portfolio. In a second phase the results of the analysis are evaluated. These results constitute the basis for the following step in the service engineering process (Figure 10).

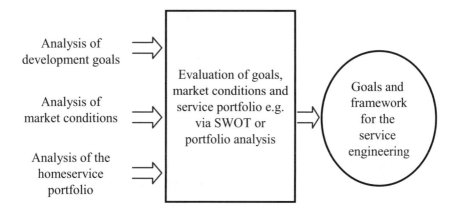

Figure 10. *Workflow and levels of analysis of a situation analysis*

The analysis of development goals refers to the goals of the providing organization. Goals of housing organizations, for instance, differ considerably and are mostly related to the purpose for which the organization was founded. In Germany, the Netherlands or Finland, for example, cities or municipalities have founded most of the housing organizations with the main goal to supply reasonably priced flats for relatively wide social strata. Therefore these organizations offer a broad variety of housing. On the contrary, for instance in Spain social housing refers only to social levels with a very low income and the organizations only offer inexpensive housing. Some of the housing organizations in Germany are joint-stock companies and their primary goal is to make a profit and they do not provide housing for all social levels, but address a middle-income clientele.

To give another example, the goals of municipal service providers supplying basically the same service may differ noticeably between countries or municipalities within one and the same country. This is because municipalities fulfil their different obligations in many ways. For example the municipal waste management company MA 48 in Vienna is responsible for waste prevention and offers a broad variety of services. It offers consultancy to individuals and business enterprises on waste prevention and waste separation, publishing a regularly updated guide on repair, rental and second-hand shops, counselling schools for education on waste matters and so on. In Germany, in contrast, municipalities often outsource waste management to private companies. These organizations are interested in a good practice of waste separation – therefore they advise consumers on harmful materials – but they are not interested in waste prevention. As a result, in some municipalities the local waste management company publishes only a small brochure on waste separation.

An analysis of the strategic goals of the relevant stakeholder (commercial and social service providers) or the legal obligations (municipalities and related companies like municipal housing organizations) can offer a basis for the service engineering process. Sources of information could be for instance corporate mission statements, legal obligations as well as interactive workshops or interviews with experts and potential customers. If there are no sustainability related goals in the organization, the lack of such goals can be one of the results of the analysis, and may lead to the question of whether such aims should be included.

The analysis of market conditions or customers needs mainly refers to the various stakeholders' incentives that relate to the provision of homeservices or could be used as a basis for the development of services in the second step of service engineering. In addition, analysing market conditions or customers needs may help to detect demands for homeservices as well as important restrictions for their supply. The macro environment, the micro environment and the situation of the company/organization are the broad factor categories to be analysed (Figure 11). Every layer and factor should be analysed with respect to the actual situation and existing trends.

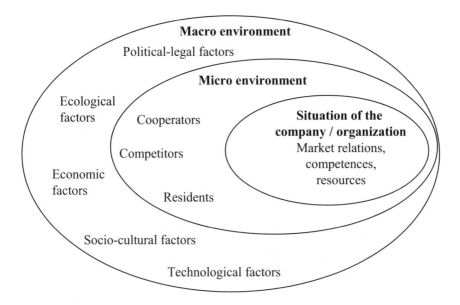

Figure 11. *Factors for the analysis of market conditions for homeservices*

For a housing organization, for instance, the macro environment includes a broad variety of factors:

- Political-legal factors: strategies for urban development, housing programs of the municipality, programs for housing and service promotion, main target groups for social housing or owner-occupancy, housing laws
- Ecological factors: trends in resource consumption and waste production, mobility, green space
- Technological factors: development of information and communication technologies, heating systems, home automation
- Socio-cultural factors: population development (single households vs. families, older people), migration
- Economic factors: local incomes, unemployment, rents.

The micro environment includes the structure and behaviour of the residents as well as the company's relationship to competitors and co-operators:

- The residents: behaviour of residents (occupancy, turnover of residents, conflicts, communication), income, demography (structure of households, social levels, age), residents' satisfaction and complaints

- Competitors and co-operators: power of competitors, target groups, cooperation between competitors, competition in the housing market, cooperation with service providers, structure and offerings of the service providers, lacks of supply.

For different types of service providers the headings will be the same but the factors change. Depending on the service provider and the service, different macro-environmental factors are relevant. It is obvious that for a service provider offering personal care services it is not important to look at strategies for urban development or ecological trends, but social-cultural and economic factors are nonetheless relevant. Therefore different kinds of service providers must adjust the factors to their own service profiles.

Within the micro environment, different target groups are relevant for different service providers. Whereas housing organizations have residents as a target group, commercial, social and municipal service providers will have another type of customer basis. For example, a delivery service for sustainable food can target customers whose motivation is to promote organic farming, whereas a social enterprise offering a similar service might have elderly and single people as their target group. The analysis of the customers must be adapted in the same way as the factors in the macro environment. In principle, the difference between housing organizations, municipal institutions, commercial or social companies is not so large. The main difference is that housing organizations have a defined target group: their residents. They can get information about their customers by resident surveys. Municipal, commercial and social service providers do not have such defined target groups and therefore their target segments should be narrowed down according to the providing organization's service profile or its goals. Especially the playing field of municipalities is changing in this respect. All over Europe there is a pressure for municipalities to cut budgets and re-organize large parts of their service supply by outsourcing or other means. On one hand more and more services, including homeservices, are being transferred from the public sector (mainly municipalities) to private enterprises or, to some extent, non-profit organizations. On the other hand municipalities are required to fill in gaps, which are not sufficiently fulfilled by social or commercial companies.

The analysis of these layers, factors and structures leads to an identification of new trends, demands or needs. On the other hand, the basic framework for the supply of services will be identified (e.g. target groups, potential co-operators, restriction in supply). Therefore the market or customer analysis contributes the factual basis for the further steps of the service engineering. As customer's demands are one of the most important factors regarding a relevant market for homeservices, customer surveys or market research can help to detect potentials – even for presently non-existent service offerings (see Chapter 3).

The concept of sustainable development can be taken into account in the analysis of market conditions in several ways. Many cities or municipalities have established goals or concepts of sustainable development. Within this framework, priority fields of action are defined. The service engineering team could use the local framework by reflecting on their organization's potential role in these fields of action. For example most of the concepts of sustainability call for a reduction of resource consumption. Within the analysis of ecological trends or the micro environment a housing organization, for example, could analyse the resource consumption (water, energy) of their residents. If there is a strong difference compared to the average resource consumption in the city, a possible starting point for service engineering has been found. A social enterprise, on the other hand, could analyse the unemployment levels and deficits of social infrastructure in areas with extensive social problems as a basis for developing new services that are based on a non-profit system and mutual aid, such as employing local unemployed residents to provide homeservices at a low or no charge for disadvantaged customers.

Moreover, service engineering should be based on a local analysis of the existing homeservice portfolio, in order to detect relevant market potentials, practices and niches. This analysis should include the actual service portfolio of the respective actor as well as homeservice offerings of comparable competitors. Within the earlier mentioned service R&D project (Hohm et al, 2004) a description of the services with respect to acceptance, strategic value and profitability turned out to be feasible.

Finally, the evaluation of the situation analysis results should summarize and assess all important factors that condition the provision of homeservices. Important factors can be distinguished from the less relevant, for instance using a SWOT analysis or a workshop. With regard to sustainable homeservice engineering, the results of the situation analysis should also reflect the precondition of sustainable development goals. For analysing the portfolio, the concept of sustainable services could be used as an evaluation tool (see Chapter 2). Using this analysis, potentially sustainable services could be identified. Services with lacking sustainability should be processed through service re-design

Step 2: Service Creation

The actual development of services starts with the service creation phase (Figure 12). The results of the situation analysis, however, form the base for this stage. The first step is to create service ideas that correspond to the detected development goals as well as to the market conditions. The choice of methods depends on the actors' preferences, that is, whether the service provider intends to create completely new services by creative processes (e.g. Brainstorming or Future Labs) or whether they explore the market potential for already existing service ideas (e.g. by scanning the literature or interviewing stakeholders). Furthermore, an analysis of customers' demands, complaints or needs could be used as initial point for the generation of ideas.

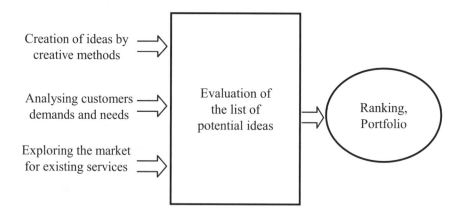

Figure 12. *Workflow of the service creation phase*

The generation of ideas for sustainable services does not differ too much from those for ordinary homeservices. Usually the search for ideas for homeservices starts with an analysis of literature ('What services are our peer organizations or competitors offering?') or with a question at a workshop (e.g. 'Do you know a service, which could fulfil the demand xyz of our customers?' or 'Do you know how we could react with a service to the main complaints of our customer?"). If the service engineering team wants to create ideas for sustainable homeservices, they should use the result of the situation analysis. For example: One of the results has been a lack of social initiatives or social responsibility of a housing organization. Therefore this gap could be used as a starting point for looking for new services. Another example: The situation analysis by a municipal actor has shown that there is a lack of short-term child-sitting. This could be a starting point for looking for new service ideas like a consultation for social companies, cooperation with housing organizations or initiatives for founding a new business. At this stage, it is not very important to concentrate only on sustainable homeservice ideas. It is much more important to generate a bundle of ideas, which will be evaluated in the next phase.

The evaluation of ideas needs a system of criteria. Because every method for generating new ideas leads to a range of ideas, the evaluation system must be easy to use. A rough screening for all kind of services or providers could be conducted, for example, using the following criteria:

- Acceptance:
  Is there a potential demand for the service?
  (+2 = large demand, -2 = low demand)
  How big is the target group?
  (+2 = big, -2 = small)
- Strategic value:
  Does the service fit the goals of the company?
  (+2 = very well, -2 = not well)
  Does the service fit the service portfolio?
  (+2 = very well, -2 = not well)
- Profitability of services:
  Will the service engender enough benefits in relation to the investment?
  (+2 = yes, -2 = no)
  How much do we have to invest?
  (+2 a lot, -2 = not so much)

The rating could be done by several rating systems, such as a scoring from -2 to +2. As a result of this stage, the most interesting ideas are identified. Table 17 illustrates an example of the rating of services for housing organizations, which was done at a workshop. In this example, all three criteria have been used including each of the six sub-criteria. Therefore a '4' indicates that the service was rated as high as possible within a criterion (modified from original examples by Jonuschat and Scharp, 2004).

Table 17. *Example of a rating of service ideas*

No.	Service ideas	Rating (average)			
		Total	Strategic value	Profitability of services	Acceptance
1	Account card	12	4	4	4
2	Virtual homeservice marketplace on the web	9	4	1	4
3	Car sharing organized by residents	9	4	3	2
4	Counselling on energy savings in cooperation with HO and energy provider	7	1	3	3
5	Counselling on energy savings by HO	7	3	1	3
6	Counselling on energy savings by residents	7	3	4	0
7	Modernization of flats for elderly residents	7	4	-1	4
8	Car sharing organized by the HO and car-sharing organization in cooperation	6	4	0	2
9	Get-together-parties for new residents	5	3	0	2
10	Move-in management	5	1	1	3
11	Multimedia service organization	-3	-1	-2	0

It is helpful to illustrate the results using a multi-dimensional graph in order to make all aspects visible. A diagram like the portfolio figure (Figure 13) makes it simple to discuss the results of the evaluation and to sort out uninteresting ideas.

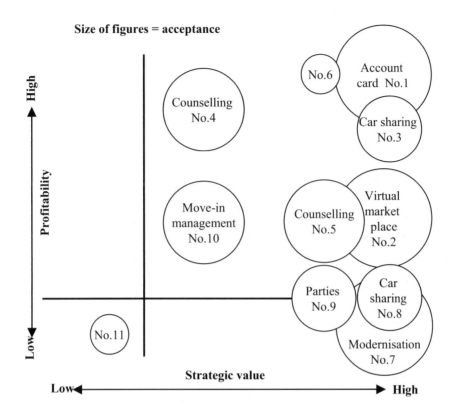

Figure 13. *Graphical ranking of service ideas*

The above-mentioned criteria are appropriate for all kinds of service providers. In the process of rating the ideas it is also possible to include sustainability criteria. If there is a long list of ideas, the service engineering team has to develop simple evaluation criteria. The criteria should reflect the main goal of developing sustainable services. For a rough evaluation and a rating it is not necessary to take the criteria of all three dimensions into account. More than three criteria are difficult to present graphically. Instead of the criteria 'strategic value' or 'profitability' used in Figure 13, the criteria related to enhancement of sustainability could be applied:

- Does the service enhance sustainability (assess separately for ecological and socio-economic dimensions)?
- Does the service fulfil important requirements of sustainability (assess separately for ecological and socio-economic dimensions)?

In this step of service engineering it is not necessary to use more detailed criteria for sustainability, but it is useful to deal with ecological and socio-economic sustainability separately, because they are qualitatively so different.

During the third phase, service design, it is possible to develop a sustainable homeservice concept, which takes into account all dimensions of sustainability. In reality, service engineering is a time-consuming process, and the first rough evaluation of ideas can be followed by a detailed evaluation using the sustainability evaluation tool (see Chapter 2). This instrument checks the ecological, economic and social impacts of the given service idea. If the goal is to develop sustainable homeservice offerings, the homeservice ideas should have mainly positive scores on all impact areas (social, economic, environment) in order to be accepted for further development in the service design phase.

Step 3: Service Design

After having created interesting service ideas, these services should be specified in detail in the service design phase. The concept of service design is identical for any type of service provider, with only minor changes. The service design process can be structured according to three concept stages (Table 18).

Table 18. *Service, process and resource concept*

What should the homeservice be?	**How** should the service be provided?	**Which** resources are available for the service?
⇩	⇩	⇩
Service concept	Process concept	Resource concept

The development of a marketing concept is a cross-section of all service design stages. The development of a marketing concept is necessary for all kinds of service providers, including municipal providers. The marketing concept is based on the marketing strategy and the so-called marketing mix. The marketing strategy determines among other things the target groups, the position of the service in the whole company performance and the internal responsibilities for marketing activities. In a traditional sense, the marketing mix includes all measures and instruments that support the supply of the service. Some components of a marketing mix are, for instance, the service, its pricing systems, sales and distribution models and promotion. These components are necessary for public and non-profit services as well, even though many of them are provided for free. Basic information for this stage should have been identified in the situation analysis, especially in the analysis of the service portfolio. More details on how the marketing concept can be included in the service design will be provided in the following sections.

Service concept

In developing the service concept, the development team first has to determine the intended performance results. The following questions may serve as a guide through the service concept design. An imaginary service provider is thinking of offering a laundry service with social and ecological sustainability benefits:

- Who is the target group of the new service idea (e.g. wealthy singles or DINKs, the elderly, or disadvantaged residents)?
- What should be offered to the target group (the variety of the services like a laundry service with home delivery, building laundrette, or building a laundrette using the '*Electrolux concept*' in which the washing machine manufacturer offers not only the machine but also installation, training, suggestions for the layout of equipment location, contracts for maintenance and repair, guarantees and financial schemes (Mont, 2004)?
- Who should offer the service (e.g. the housing organization by itself, the housing organization in cooperation with another service provider or a laundry service provider alone)?

As a result of these questions, a rough idea of the possible services together with their target groups and ways of offering the service becomes more concrete. Furthermore – as a part of the marketing concept – the pricing system needs to be given due consideration. Without knowing the processes and the involvement of personnel and resources, the costs of a service can only be estimated by a comparison of market prices in relation to the possibilities of the customers. Especially social services are mostly restricted by the income of the customers. Even if the service will be offered for free by a social or municipal provider, a marketing concept should be developed and a price limit should be set. Furthermore marketing goals have to be established. Without having a goal it is useless to design a service. Moreover, without having an idea of what the result of a sustainable homeservice should be, it is not possible to establish a sustainable service. Therefore every goal must be connected to indicators enabling an assessment of the effects of the (sustainable) service (see section 'service management' later in this chapter).

After determining an interesting target group, customer demands should be analysed in order to increase the potential acceptance of the service. One relevant instrument to include customer demands in the service design process and provide a basis for the marketing concept is the so-called Kano model, which distinguishes between threshold, performance and excitement attributes (Kano et al,1996). The Kano model proposes that there are certain 'threshold attributes', which are the expected attributes or 'musts' of a service. Customers are not prepared to pay extra for threshold attributes. The 'performance attributes' on the other hand are the core aspects of a service, as a good performance improves the customer satisfaction, while a weak one reduces it. Moreover, the customers' willingness to pay is closely connected to the performance attributes. Thirdly 'excitement attributes' are unexpected by the customers but can result in a high customer satisfaction, although their absence does not lead to dissatisfaction. Relating generally to still latent demands and no direct needs, excitement attributes are an important competitive factor in some services. Excitement attributes are not important for all kinds of services, and one should consider carefully whether a social or municipal service needs such attributes. Especially in the case of services provided free of charge, it may be necessary to abandon excitement attributes to reduce the cost of the service.

The Kano model can be applied, for instance, in customer surveys or focus groups in order to determine important service features or subtypes of services (e.g. providing building laundrette, making it more comfortable with windows to the garden or a playing corner for children, offering additional laundry service) that must or should be included in the service design process. On the basis of the customer demand analysis, the service designers can specify the performance and prepare a descriptive service model by combining features (see below). Furthermore the acceptance of the pricing system can be tested in the discussions with potential customers. Service providers – including housing organizations – should be aware that many customers would like to have services, but only specific segments of them are likely to pay more than a moderate cost, unless the service is very necessary for them (for further discussion on willingness to pay for homeservices see Chapters 2 and 5).

The next step of the service design is combining the features of the service and the Kano attributes. An evaluation using the Quality Function Method can be made with the help of a simple matrix of features (columns) and attributes (lines). Rating factors could range from zero (not important) to three (very important). To highlight important attributes, multiplication (weighting) factors can be used. The sum of every column indicates the importance of a service feature or subtype of a service. Table 19 illustrates the outcome of a rating example based the Quality Function Method (QFM).

Table 19. *Evaluation of 'laundry / washing service' using the QFM*

Kano attributes (Customer demand)	Weighting factors	Service features (not weighted and weighted)											
		Standard, nw	Standard, w	Pickup and delivery, nw	Pickup and delivery, w	Consultation, nw	Consultation, w	Emergency aid, nw	Emergency aid, w	Biological cleaning, nw	Biological cleaning, w	Tailoring service, nw	Tailoring service, w
Cheap	3	9	27										
No fogging	3									9	27		
Easy hand over	2			9	18								
Quick	2			9	18			9	18				
More than washing; 'ready-to wear'	1			3	3	3	3	3	3	3	3	9	9
Advice	2			3	6	9	18					3	6
Sum of rows			27		45		21		21		30		15
Priority			3		1		4		4		2		5

Abbreviations: nw = not weighted; w = weighted; standard = only chemical cleaning

The result of the service concept is a detailed description of the homeservice in terms of its features or of identifiable subtypes of the service. Customer demands as a part of the marketing concept have also been included.

Sustainability considerations come into the design table primarily when the second question, what service should be offered, is to be answered. By answering this question the service idea is roughly outlined. While answering, it is possible to optimize the service idea with regard to sustainability. For example, if the first idea was the rental of dishes, it could be made more concrete in respect to sustainability if the rental service excludes one-way dishes. The rental of dishes could furthermore be combined with the delivery of organic food snacks. Or there could be a cooperation with a social initiative, delivering the leftover food to a shelter for the homeless. It is possible to include even further sustainability goals. Maybe a housing organization has asserted in the situation analysis that it needs to improve social contacts. The idea of 'renting dishes' could be extended to setting up a party service offered by the housing organization's own residents.

Thus, by roughly characterizing a service idea, we have substantiated the idea step by step, and were able to include sustainability aspects. Outlining an idea in this way relates to one of the most important points about sustainability: it is not a ready concept, but a process of looking forward or a continual search for better alternatives. The criteria of sustainable services (Chapter 2) can be used as a baseline for this process, against which every idea has to be reflected.

Process concept

The next step is the modelling of the processes. With regard to modelling any service process, it is helpful to define four phases:

1. Sales and distribution (e.g. via internet, service centre),
2. Provision processes (e.g. reservation, accounting, delivery),
3. Service assessment (e.g. recording of complaints, employees' amendments).
4. Supply of physical components of the service (e.g. common rooms, equipment, information brochures, website).

The core component of the process concept is to mark out the processes that mainly determine sales and distribution, provision and assessment. Within this step the distribution module of the marketing concept has to be shaped. Physical components are inasmuch part of the process concept as they are the basis for most of the processes. For example: Nearly every kind of homeservice has to do something with transport activities. Therefore the means of transport should be considered: bicycle, electric car, ordinary car, public transport or other? To develop the process concept the engineering team can start with sales and distribution as well as with the provision processes. All processes must always be separated into single activities, but it is easier to start with the provision processes, because sales and distribution assessments are based on the provision processes.

For example in the first step the question 'How does a customer get the service?' is to be answered. There are several possibilities from e-mail or phone call to paying a visit to the service provider's office. The next step is the question: Will the request be sent to a service provider, will the service provider be informed by the office or does the office inform its own staff? If the engineering team starts with sales and distribution, the first question could be 'How can we make our customer aware of and interested in the service?' Possible answers could be an advertisement on the announcement board, distributing flyers to apartments or using the web page. Further questions relate to the coordination of the customer and the supplier, the assessment of the service or the method of payment.

All these activities can be illustrated by a so-called blueprint that visualizes activities according to actors and stages of interaction (external interaction with the customer = line 1; the internal interactions of the service providers = line 2). Figure 14 represents a blueprinting for a repair service, which will be administrated in cooperation between a service and a repair centre. Line 1 represents the line of external interaction between the customer and the housing organization / repair centre, line 2 represents the line of internal interaction between the housing organization and the repair centre. It is possible to draw a third line between these two lines, which represent the line of visibility. All interaction up to this line are visible for the customer, all interaction below this line are not visible for the customer.

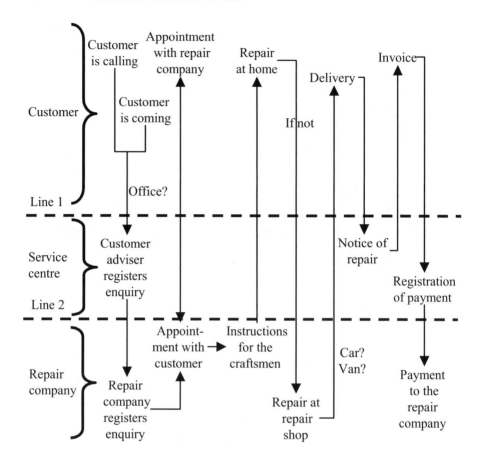

Figure 14. *Outline of the processes of a repair service*

Integrating sales and distribution activities as well as service assessment activities can complement the process blueprinting. By dividing the whole service into individual activities, they also demonstrate clearly where physical infrastructure is needed. The process concept is more or less independent of the service provider.

The process concept could be used to design the processes according to the standards of sustainability. For example it is well accepted that mobility is one of the important fields of action to reduce emissions. Taking this and other known requirements into account can help to design a sustainable homeservice. Therefore a potential cooperation should include a strategy to minimize emissions, for example by small and modern freight vehicles. Other possible features which make the repair service more sustainable could be the following: upgrading of old household equipment, environmentally friendly waste disposal, integrating handicapped craftsmen in the repair service, indexed prices, etc. For making a service more sustainable it is helpful to use the criteria of a sustainable service and to check for every process step whether there are possibilities to make the service more sustainable (cf. Chapter 2).

Resource concept

Finally, the service designers must detect relevant resources for the concept. The resource concept comprises the choice and qualifications of the staff and the supply of physical and financial resources as well as potential ICT applications. Furthermore the promotion of the service as the last part of the marketing concept needs to be outlined.

One possibility to outline a resource concept uses tables that list all the necessary resources according to the lifecycle phases. Table 20 illustrates a resource matrix for a workshop room with tool sharing. The service was provided by a housing organization in cooperation with the residents.

Table 20. *Resource matrix of a workshop room and tool sharing service*

	Staff			Company resources			ICT	
	Own staff	External staff	Residents	Room in	Financials	...	Internet	Hotline
Supply of physical components								
- Choice of workshop room	X			X				
- Choice of equipment of workshop room			X		X			
-								
Sales and distribution								
- Information on homepage		X			X		X	
- Article in resident newspapers	X							
- Payment method (e.g. monthly dues)	X							
- ...								

Table 20. *Continued*

	Staff			Company resources			ICT	
	Own staff	External staff	Residents	Room in	Financials	...	Internet	Hotline
Provision processes								
- Reservation			X					
- Key deposit			X					
-								
Service assessment								
- Recording and treatment of complaints	X						X	X
- Check-up of room and tools			X					
- Maintenance and repairs of tools		X			X			

However, such a resource matrix can only give a broad overview of the relevant aspects that have to be considered in service provision. In general, resources must be continually adapted to the actual demand after implementation.

Aspects of sustainability can be included into the resource concept as well. Maybe the service design has led to a cleaning service for elderly people, which involves unemployed residents of a housing organization. Therefore two important dimensions for the company have been considered. Nevertheless it is possible to make the service much more sustainable if the cleaning is done with biodegradable detergents. Furthermore, the service could be improved if the cleaning service could use deposit rooms at the houses to avoid transporting materials. This example indicates that it is very helpful if the resources and the processes of the services are well known. A homeservice by itself is seldom either sustainable or unsustainable. But a service can always be improved and most importantly, changed into a sustainable service.

Evaluation of the product, process, resource and marketing concept

As mentioned above, characterizing the design concept and modelling the process and the resource concept are relevant with regard to sustainability effects. They include ecological and social impacts relating to sales and distribution as well as to the provision processes. Moreover, physical components that often have considerable environmental effects are planned during this engineering phase. Therefore, the sustainability assessment tool (Table 21) can be a helpful instrument to check every decision during the service design. But it can also be used twice. On the one hand, it can be used as a checklist to reflect the most important criteria of a sustainable service. On the other hand it can be used as an instrument to distinguish between different ways of providing the service.

Table 21. *Set of indicators for evaluating the sustainable performance of homeservices*

Environmental aspects	Social Aspects	Economic Aspects
1 Material use	7 Equity	14 Employment
2 Energy use	8 Health	15 Financial situation of the residents
3 Water use	9 Safety and security	16 Regional product and service use
4 Waste	10 Comfort	17 Profitability for the company
5 Emissions	11 Social contacts	18 Profitability for the region / community
6 Space use	12 Empowerment	
	13 Information and awareness	

Step 4: Service Management

Service management as a service engineering phase comprises the implementation of the service in the market as well as a long-term assessment. The implementation of the homeservice consists in managing the institutional arrangement as well as in integrating the service in company operation structures. The long-term assessment can be divided into evaluation processes regarding profitability, acceptance and strategic goals – such as sustainable development in this case. In this last subchapter only a few aspects of sustainability will be outlined in the context of service management.

Service implementation

With regard to sustainability effects, institutional arrangements can have various impacts. Firstly, a single-handed supply by the housing organization or service provider results in sole responsibility for sustainability effects regarding the service content and logistics. Consequently the supplier can, for instance, decide on developing a sustainable food delivery service by optimising sustainability effects by using bicycles for delivery and favouring organic food from regional suppliers. In contrast, cooperation is based on shared responsibilities between both partners. The providing organization can therefore influence sustainability effects by optimising its own contribution and choosing suitable partners that also follow sustainability strategies. Finally, with regard to residents' or customers' involvement (typically for services of social enterprises and housing organizations), the initiating institution has an influence on the general concept of service provision. So, for example, a housing organization that forms a tenants' association in order to organize a swap shop contributes to sustainable development goals by initiating a non-profit, material saving service offering, although the service itself is carried out by the residents.

Service assessment

The long-term service assessment aims at the continuous improvement of the service performance. Hereby, there are three main aspects that should be taken into consideration while assessing the service's performance: profitability, acceptance and sustainability effects. The profitability of the service can be evaluated by implementing a continuous control of the service costs and of its use by the customers. The profitability assessment also involves issues such as the examination of provision processes or staff expenses.

Moreover, customer surveys can give information on service acceptance. Another way is to analyse the complaints of customers. Furthermore, the employees involved can often give additional information on the acceptance of the service. The results of analysing the acceptance should always form the basis for a re-design of the service.

Last but not least, the sustainability effects of the service should be assessed. The service assessment is based on the indicators established in the design concept. A service can be designed to enhance sustainability in many ways. For example, a joint labour project of an NPO and a housing organization aiming at reducing unemployment in a neighbourhood by offering home-services conducted by the unemployed people will fulfil only one of 18 indicators if the unemployed people are employed. But if, for example, low-income elderly people can ask for assistance for free, or if some of the offered services have environmental features, the sustainability profile becomes more comprehensive. Therefore the service design must establish the criteria for the service, which can be used at this point to assess the service.

7 Rediscovering immaterial pleasure

The aspiration of this book was to find answers to the question of why eco-efficient or sustainable services are not more popular in the consumer market, and explore ideas for making them more attractive for consumers. For some years, the evidence has been mounting that services designed for sustainability could be one of the feasible ways to reduce the environmental burden caused by the affluent societies, without people having to sacrifice the fulfilment of their needs. This approach has worked relatively successfully in business-to-business services, but consumer services keep staggering. It appears that the present infrastructures and institutions often tend to favour material-intensive forms of consumption, many symbolic values are related to the ownership of products, and many times even those consumers who would be interested in using services for sustainability are unaware of them. This list of obstacles sounds rather desperate, but on the other hand there are also positive trends that can support the sustainable consumer service approach if correctly utilised, as we could see in this book. It takes a fair amount of time and effort to change institutions, infrastructures and dominant consumption mentalities, and such a shift will not come from one single source but from many little streams. Some steps are possible already now.

There are already providers and users of sustainable consumer services – and many more opportunities for different types of providers to discover. However, there is a need to rethink who the potential providers are, as well as what the main incentives are for consumers to use services enhancing sustainability. The dominant approach is to try to persuade large companies to offer sustainable consumer services and to expect that consumers will be convinced to use them because of environmental concerns or the economic rationale of saving money. This is not a comprehensive understanding of the situation. What, then, would be more accurate conceptions and how and with whom can sustainable service promoters continue to work for a more sustainable future? In this chapter we highlight some selected findings and ideas, but they do not form a complete summary of the book. For that purpose, it is best to read the concluding sections of each chapter.

BUSINESS FOR MULTIPLE PROVIDERS

"Having a car can be such pain in the a-- for a woman. First your exhaust pipe breaks down, then a tyre goes flat or the engine just won't start. I don't like to feel like a helpless woman, because that's not me, I'm not helpless. The very day my housing organization contracted a car-sharing company's car in the front of my building, I went for the service. I'd rather outsource these problems to my car-sharing organization and move instead of getting stuck in my very own steel box."

The evidence in this book shows that the quality of consumers' everyday life deserves more attention in the eco-efficiency research and design practice, and moreover, that the provider questions need to be understood more profoundly, if realistic solutions are to come about. If consumers are to use services compensating products, they need to be as easily accessible as owned products. One of the implications is that services ought to be offered directly at home or near to it. But how to accomplish this in a cost-efficient fashion? For whom does it make sense to offer sustainable services to consumers at their home or in the vicinity?

Often when thinking about sustainable services, we tend to assume that new enterprises should miraculously appear to provide such services, or we expect that large corporations adopt product-service systems that enhance sustainable development. These assumptions are not incorrect but they are incomplete. The array of sustainable consumer services is vast. Different services attract different providers just like service needs and wants differ between consumer segments. Sustainable or potentially sustainable household services are offered by a variety of providers from SMEs, non-profit organizations or public sector service providers to housing organizations, housing management companies and large companies, and they all should be adequately taken into account in eco-efficient service research and development.

One relevant actor group is completely missing from the sustainable service discussion. Housing organizations are in many instances a natural agent to provide services or act as an intermediary for homeservices – and the pioneering ones actually already do so. They provided one-fifth of the 200 services studied under the auspices of this book. Housing organizations and housing management companies bear close proximity to the consumers, the residents, and hence have the opportunity to provide services directly to the residents in their homes. From the consumers' viewpoint, proximity means that services can be acquired as easily as products fulfilling the same need, which is one of the main conditions for consumers to replace or supplement their product-based consumption with services. The business benefit for housing organizations is that services increase tenant loyalty, which in turn promotes longer tenancies and reduces negligence and vandalism, both of which lead to indirect cost savings for housing organizations. Housing management or maintenance companies, on the other hand, offer additional services if they can use them to generate new business.

"Did you ever drag your broken b ike on the bus and metro to a repair store? I'm all sweaty and have just about had enough of the angry looks, too. Why is it always others that have the nice things around, like... can you imagine this, a housing organization that arranges a mobile bicycle m echanic to visit the building and do a spring repair of the tenants' bicycles? I'd gladly pay a couple of more euros to a bike mechanic who comes to my place than take this annoyance."

Often it does not make sense for the housing operators to produce household services by themselves. Housing organizations and housing management companies are at present an under-utilised marketing channel for services. Various service companies could win new business opportunities by cooperating with them in service provision.

Apart from housing organizations, there are other considerations concerning service providers. As contended above, for some providers it makes more sense to provide certain services than other ones. What service types are feasible for which providers? One of the service clusters identified in the previous chapters was 'ordinary services with eco-features' (delivery of organic food, eco-gardening etc, see Chapter 2). These services appear to be most often provided by relatively small business enterprises. More complex service concepts call for collaboration by a variety of providers spanning from business enterprises to public sector organizations. This is the case for services that require information, knowledge, contacts, access to certain infrastructural resources or other forms of support such as capital input from other than the central provider. For instance a number of energy saving services or 'multiple services from the same counter' introduced earlier in this book are such concepts.

On the other hand some services in some situations are best and most (eco)efficiently provided by the public sector or non-profit organizations. This is the case especially when the infrastructures and institutions, such as for instance municipal libraries or free school lunches in the Nordic countries, already exist. Unsexy, isn't it? But it is about time that we analyse efficiency objectively case by case and see that it is not the sole domain of business enterprises. When well-organized, public provision can be efficient, too.

Social enterprises for their part are suitable particularly for homeservices that are labour-intensive, but do not require high technical skills. They are an excellent vehicle for offering unknown or untested services that are considered too risky or uninteresting by commercial enterprises because of the difficulty to foresee whether there will be a profitable demand. From the sustainability perspective, more often than not, social enterprises offer environmentally conscious services. As to social sustainability, they offer employment to people who would not otherwise be able to enter the job market. This is economically beneficial because society saves money by not having to support unemployment. Instead, it gains employment opportunities and the ensuing benefits with lesser financial support.

But whoever the provider of the service, the business model of the service deserves careful attention. This means scrutinising the benefits that customers can derive from the service (compared to more material intensive ways of fulfilling their needs), the competitive advantage that pertains to it, the capabilities and resources needed by the provider or providers, and the financing arrangements.

The above is not to say that all services by definition are sustainable. It is always a matter of the service design. A simple set of criteria that can be applied for developing new services as well as for improving existing ones is presented in Chapter 6.

MAKING SERVICE USE EASIER

"I'm busy. I have the money, but no time at all. I use services for every possible domestic task that you can name, but there is one problem. Finding reliable providers easily eats up my few free moments – let alone if someone causes trouble, which I must deal with later on. But as I always say, when there is a problem, there is also a solution. In my case it is the virtual homeservice marketplace. It's my cup of tea: one click, and in two seconds you are among 400 service providers from mobile catering and cleaning to repair services making house calls. Swindlers sorted out."

The ability of services to improve their users' quality of life of – "user pleasure" – is a crucial determinant for the competitiveness of services in the market place. Both the consumer survey (Chapter 3) as well as the evaluation of real-life sustainable household services (Chapter 2) indicate that especially the ability of a service to add comfort for the users has been given inadequate attention in eco-efficient service research and development. In this context 'comfort' does not primarily refer to luxury – rather, it materialises for ordinary people in such things as time saving or smoother running of everyday life.

Potential markets for household services are offered by trends such as the aging population that needs services to continue living at home, time constraints of working families and a segment of single people wishing to outsource some of their domestic tasks. From the supply perspective, developments in ICTs have made it possible to offer some services at a lower cost. This potential is, however, counteracted by lack of information about homeservices among the potential users and, secondly, the fact that those in need of services are often not used to using them, or cannot afford them. To reach these potential customers, different strategies are called for. For customers who could afford to pay for services, but for attitudinal reasons do not use them, strategies aiming at attitude change are called for. Attitudes can be changed to some degree by making homeservices available so easily that pioneering customers start to use them, setting a model for others to follow. This is likely to pave the way for more service-based consumption patterns. One way to promote availability is to bundle the offer of several household services together. If a potential customer can get services via one phone number or a well-designed website (such as some Austrian housing organizations' service centres, Buenos Dias/Buenas Noches, the ELIAS virtual market place for homeservices in Chapter 2), it is more likely that services will be used. For instance the fact that repair services for household appliances are so difficult to find means that consumers are much more inclined to just buy a new appliance rather than have even minor faults fixed. It is also possible to specifically craft eco-efficiency into these concepts (see ELIAS virtual marketplace in Chapter 2).

On the other hand, for those who are in need of homeservices, but cannot afford them, strategies should primarily aim at finding suitable financing structures. In the latter instances, cooperation of the public sector and NPOs or social enterprises may offer feasible solutions.

"My wife kept nagging about the heat. She went on and on telling me that I'm no man if I can't fix a couple of radiators. I admit that 26 degrees indoors sort of makes you nervous, but what could I do? Then my wife spotted that our housing organization had appointed an 'energy expert', one of my neighbours. First I was suspicious about the 'know-it-all energy expert guy', but he did plenty of good stuff in our flat. No more tipping taps or leaking radiators, and new thermostats... Besides, who'd think that your wife fancies you better in a lower temperature?"

Individual people or households are seldom perfectly free to choose their consumption forms. Depending on the consumption cluster (such as nutrition, mobility, housing), households alone have only limited – greater or lesser, but still limited – possibilities to influence their patterns of consumption. There are always other actors who are relevant in setting the frame for consumption choices. For instance with regard to housing and construction, property owners (housing providers), local authorities and service providers influence the housing framework (e.g. form of heating and the like are seldom a free consumer choice). Or as regards mobility, local authorities and service providers have a lot to do with the transport infrastructure (such as public transport or bicycle lanes), and consequently they set the limits within which consumers are able to decide how to fulfil their housing and mobility needs. Therefore it is important that housing and mobility providers, for instance, arrange the conditions so that it is as easy as possible for households to organize their daily lives as sustainably as possible.

HAPPINESS SOLUTIONS

"It's funny, really, to enjoy doing the laundry. I take my kids down to the house laundrette on the ground floor, set them playing with toys in the kids' corner and stuff the dirty laundry into the washing machine. When I close the washing room door behind me, the voice of the machine becomes likes a humming at the background. Then I go to the coffee machine, and take a cup. In the best case one of my neighbours is there, and I can ha ve a few adult words with someone. These are the peaceful moments of the day, gazing out at the garden from the laundry room window, seeing the kids play out of the corner of my eye, sipping coffee."

The above vignettes are not here only to amuse us. They remind us that most people do not use services in order to protect the environment. They may not even use them to save money or for other evidently rational reasons. All kinds of unexpected motives may lie behind (sustainable) service use, and these reasons may strongly vary between individuals. Understanding the different motivations requires a fair amount of more knowledge than we have yet. There is, however, one common denominator in our behaviours. We all seek for moments of happiness and pleasure in our everyday lives.

Recently happiness has been (re)discovered even within economics (Layard, 2005). Economists are now able to show with empirical evidence what many of us know from experience or by intuition: After a certain basic level, material wealth does not make people any happier (Layard, 2005), but perhaps the contrary (Hamilton, 2003). And economists are not the leading idealists. If they are ready to admit that material wealth does not equal happiness, then a good part of the materially saturated Western world probably is ready for that message. The question for sustainable service promoters then is, whether to connect the service approach to the happiness discourse more compellingly, making use of the emotional leverage, which at present is commonly treated as an unavoidable problem in the eco-efficiency and product-service-systems discussions. Perhaps the often-used 'customer is emotional' notion of the product-service systems discourse can be turned into a solution rather than a problem, as it is often currently framed. The ecological and efficiency facts are known, but they do not seem to turn the heads of many. Rather than following the beaten track of rational argumentation, should sustainable consumer services be portrayed as sources of pleasurable every day life? And how to accomplish that?

'Poetry may work where facts fail'. The power of story telling has been understood within the eco-efficiency community. The problem is, however, that the story types applied, techno-utopias or resource-conserving scenarios, will not hit most people's emotional cords. Understanding the ways in which sustainable services may help or be in line with the pursuit of happiness – and communicating it, 'telling the good stories of everyday life' – may just be the next step for sustainable service providers, designers and researchers to take.

What's your story?

References

Chapter 1

Baron, S. and Harris, K. (2003) *Services Marketing: Text and Cases*, Houndmills, Palgrave

Behrendt, S., Kortman, J. and Jasch, C., Hrauda, G. and Velte, D. (2003) *Eco-Service Development: Reinventing Supply and Demand in the European Union*, Sheffield, Greenleaf Publishing

Bell, D. (1976) *The Coming of Post-Industrial Society,* Harmondsworth, Penguin Books

Gatersleben, B. (2001) 'Sustainable Household Consumption and Quality of Life: The Acceptability of Sustainable Consumption Patterns and Consumer Policy Strategies', *International Journal of Environment and Pollution*, vol 15, no 2, pp 200–216

Gatersleben, B. and Vlek., Ch. (1998) 'Household Consumption, Quality of Life, and Environmental Impacts: A Psychological Perspective and Empirical Study', in Noorman, K. and Uiterkamp, T. (eds.) *Green Households? Domestic Consumers, Environment and Sustainability,* London, Earthscan

Goedkoop, M.J., van Halen, C., te Riele, H. and Rommels, P., (1999). *Product-service Systems, Ecological and Economic Basics*, The Hague, Ministry of Housing, Spatial Planning and the Environment

Heiskanen, E. (2001) 'Review of the Discussion on Eco-efficient Services', in Heiskanen, E., Halme, M., Jalas, M., Kärnä, A. and Lovio, R. *Dematerialization: the Potential of ICT and Services*, Helsinki, Ministry of the Environment 533

Heiskanen, E. and Jalas, M. (2003) 'Can Services Lead to Radical Eco-efficiency Improvements? – Review of the Debate and Evidence', *Corporate Social Responsibility and Environmental Management* vol10, pp186–198

Hobson, K. (2002) 'Competing Discourses of Sustainable Consumption: Does the 'Rationalization of Lifestyles' Make Sense?', *Environmental Politics*, vol 11, no 2, pp95–120

Hockerts, K. (1999) 'Innovation of Eco-Efficient Services: Increasing the Efficiency of Products and Services', in Charter, M. and Polonsky, J. (eds.) *Greener Marketing: A Global Perspective on Greening Marketing Practice* , Sheffield, Greenleaf Publishing

Hrauda, G., Jasch, C., Kranzl, S. and Horvath, F. (2002) *Homeservices aus der Fabrik der Zukunft,* Endbericht, Eigenverlag des IÖW Wien, Schriftenreihe 30/02 Available also at www.ioew.at/ioew/download/Endbericht_homeservice.pdf./ accessed in December 2003

Hukkinen, J. (2003) 'From Groundless Universalism to Grounded Generalism: Improving Ecological Economic Indicators of Human-environmental Interaction', *Ecological Economics,* vol 44, pp11–27

Jalas, M. (2002) 'A Time Use Perspective on the Materials Intensity of Consumption', *Ecological Economics*, vol 41, pp109–123

Jänicke, M., Mönch, H., Ranneberg, T. and Simonis, U. (1989) 'Structural Change and Environmental Impact: Empirical Evidence on Thirty-one Countries in East and West', *Environmental Monitoring and Assessment*, vol 12, pp99–114

Lovins, A., Lovins, L.H. and Hawken, P. (1999) 'A Road-map to Natural Capitalism', *Harvard Business Review*, May-June, pp145–158

McMakin, A., Malone, E. and Lundgren, R. (2002) 'Motivating Residents to Conserve Energy Without Financial Incentives', *Environment and Behaviour*, vol 34, no 6, pp848–863

Mont, O. (2002) 'Clarifying the Concept of Product-service System', *Journal of Cleaner Production*, vol 10, no 3, pp237–254

Payne, A. (1993) *The Essence of Services Marketing*, London, Prentice Hall

Peattie, K. (2001) 'Golden Goose or Wild Goose? The Hunt for the Green Consumer', *Business Strategy and the Environment*, vol 10, no 4, pp187–199

Roy, R. (2000) 'Sustainable Product-service Systems', *Futures*, vol 32, pp289–299

Salzman, J. (2000) 'Environmental Protection Beyond the Smokestack: Addressing the Impact of the Service Economy', *Corporate Environmental Strategy*, vol 7, no 1, pp20–37

Sanne, C. (2002) 'Willing Consumers – or Locked-in? Policies for Sustainable Consumption', *Ecological Economics*, vol 42, pp273–287

Scharp, M., Galonska, J. and Knoll, M. (2000) Benchmarking in der Wohnungs- und Immobilienwirtschaft – Entwicklung einer Balanced Scorecard, Berlin, IZT-Werkstattbericht 53

Schmidt-Bleek, F. (1998) *Das MIPS-Konzept. Weniger Naturverbrauch – mehr Lebensqualität durch Faktor 10*, Muenchen, Droemer Knaur

Shostack, G.L. (1977) 'Breaking Free from Product Marketing', *Journal of Marketing*, April, pp73–80

Spangenberg, J. and Lorek, S. (2002) 'Environmentally Sustainable Household Consumption: From Aggregate Environmental Pressures to Priority Fields of Action', *Ecological Economics*, vol 43, pp127–140

SusProNet (2003) 'The Product/Service Systems Network', www.suspronet.org/ accessed in May 2003

Tukker, A. (2004) 'Eight Types of Product-service-systems: Eight Ways to Sustainability? Experiences from SusProNet', *Business Strategy and the Environment*, July-August, pp246–260

Turner, K. (1998) 'Household Metabolism in the Context of Sustainability and Environmental Quality', in Noorman, K. and Uiterkamp, T. (eds.) *Green Households? Domestic Consumers, Environment and Sustainability*, London, Earthscan

Vergragt, P. (2000) *Strategies Toward Sustainable Households.* Final report of the SusHouse project. University of Delft, Faculty of Technology, Policy and Management

von Weizäcker, E., Lovins, A. and Lovins, L.H. (1997). *Factor Four: Doubling Wealth, Halving Resource use*, London, Earthscan

World Commission on Environment and Development (WCED) (1987) *Our Common Future*, Oxford, Oxford University Press

Zeithaml, V. and Bitner, M.J. (1996) *Services Marketing*, New York, Mc.Graw-Hill

Chapter 2

'Aylesbury Vale Waste Reduction in Industry', Final Report (2002) www.oakdenehollins.co.uk/pdf/final_report_2002.pdf/ accessed in March 2004

Bentley, M.D. and de Leeuw, B. (2003) 'Sustainable Consumption Indicators', http://greenplanet.eolss.net/EolssLogn/default.htm./ accessed in November 2003

Dovers, S. (1995) 'A Framework for Scaling and Framing Policy Problems in Sustainability', *Ecological Economics*, vol 12, pp93–106

Emmaus International (2005) www.emaus.com/ accessed in June 2005

Gatersleben, B. (2001) 'Sustainable Household Consumption and Quality of Life: The Acceptability of Sustainable Consumption Patterns and Consumer Policy Strategies', *International Journal of Environment and Pollution*, vol 15, no 2, pp200–216

Halme, M, Jasch, C. and Scharp, M. (2004a) 'Sustainable Homeservices? Toward Household Services that Enhance Ecological, Social and Economic Sustainability' *Ecological Economics*, vol 51, pp125–138.

Halme, M, Hrauda, G, Jasch, C, Jonuschat, H, Kortman, J Trindade, P and Velte, D. (2004b) '*Sustainable Homeservices: Benchmarking Sustainable Services for the Housing Sector for the City of Tomorrow*'. Scientific report to the European Union, available at www.sustainable-homeservices.com.

Halme, M. and Anttonen, M. (2004) 'Sustainable Homeservice Report for Finland', www.sustainable-homeservices.com/scifi-bg-set.html/

Heiskanen, E. (2001) 'Review of the Discussion on Eco-efficient Services', in Heiskanen, E., Halme, M., Jalas, M., Kärnä, A. and Lovio, R. *Dematerialization: the Potential of ICT and Services* , Helsinki, Ministry of the Environment 533

Heiskanen, E. and Jalas, M. (2003) 'Can Services Lead to Radical Eco-efficiency Improvements? – Review of the Debate and Evidence', *Corporate Social Responsibility and Environmental Management* vol10, pp186–198

Hockerts, K. (1999) 'Innovation of Eco-efficient services: Increasing the Efficiency of Products and Services', in Charter, M. and Polonsky, J. (eds.) *Greener Marketing: A Global Perspective on Greening Marketing Practice*, Sheffield, Greenleaf Publishing

Hohm, D., Hoppe, A., Jonuschat, H., Scharp, M., Scheer, D. and Scholl, G. (2002) *Dienstleistungen in der Wohnungwirtschaft: Professionelle Entwicklund neuer Serviceangebote* , Dokumentation des Workshops, Berlin, Institut für ökologische Wirtschaftsforschung (IÖW) gGmbH, 11 November

Lehtonen, M. (2004) 'The Environmental-social Interface of Sustainable Development: Capababilities, Social capital, Institutions'. *Ecological Economics* vol 49, pp199–214

Lorek, S. (2002) *Indicators for Environmentally Sound Household Consumption*, Paper presented at the Workshop on Lifecycle Approaches to Sustainable Consumption. Laxenburg, Austria, November 22

Lorek, S. and Spangenberg, J. (2001) Environmentally Sustainable Household Consumption: From Aggregate Environmental Pressures to Indicators for Priority Fields of Action, Wuppertal Papers no 117, www.wupperinst.org/Sites/wp.html accessed in December 2003

Mannis, A (1998) 'Indicators of Sustainable Development', www.ess.co.at/GAIA/Reports/indics.html./ accessed in February 2003.

OECD (1999) 'Towards more Sustainable Household Consumption Patterns: Indicators to Measure progress', Environment Directorate, www.olis.oecd.org/olis/1998doc.nsf/linkto/env-epoc-se(98)2-final./ accessed in November 2002

OECD (2001) 'Round Table on Sustainable Development: Measuring What?', Background paper for the OECD Round Table on Sustainable Development, www.oecd.org/dataoecd/9/47/2731186.pdf./ accessed in November 2002

Scharp, M., Galonska, J. and Knoll, M. (2000) Benchmarking in der Wohnungs- und Immobilienwirtschaft – Entwicklung einer Balanced Scorecard, Berlin, IZT-Werkstattbericht 53

Sen, A. (1999) *Development as Freedom*, New York, Anchor Books

Spangenberg, J. and Lorek, S. (2002) 'Environmentally Sustainable Household Consumption: From Aggregate Environmental Pressures to Priority Fields of Action', *Ecological Economics*, vol 43, pp127–140

United Nations Development Program (UNDP) (2001) *Human Development Report 2001: Making New Technologies Work for Human Development*, Oxford, Oxford University Press, available also at: www.undp.org/hdr2001/front.pdf./

United Nations Division for Sustainable Development (UNDSD) (2002) 'Indicators of Sustainable Development: Guidelines and Methodologies', www.un.org/esa/sustdev/isd.htm./ accessed in December 2002

Vercalsteren, A. and Gerken, T. (2004) *Suspronet Report WP11: Need Area Households*, August, www.suspronet.org/fs_reports.htm, accessed September 2004

Wolf, S. and Allen, T. (1995) 'Recasting Alternative Agriculture as a Management Model: The Value Adapt Scaling', *Ecological Economics*, vol 12, pp5–12

Chapter 3

Ahlqvist, K., Heiskanen, E., Huovinen, E. and Maljonen E. (2004) 'Future Lifestyles of Consumers and the Acceptability of Eco-efficient Innovations', (in Finnish), National Consumer Research Centre, www.kuluttajatutkimuskeskus.fi./ accessed in February 2005

Behrendt, S., Kortman, J., Jasch, C., Hrauda, G. and Velte, D. (2003) *Eco-service Development: Reinventing Supply and Demand in the European Union*, Sheffield, Greenleaf Publishing

Bosch, G. (1997) 'Bildung, Innovation und Chancengleichheit auf dem Arbeitsmarkt', in Institut Arbeit und Technik: Jahrbuch 1996/97, pp10–27, Gelsenkirchen

Bundesverband Gas und Wasser (2003), 'Abwasser', www.bundesverband-gas-und-wasser.de/bgw/abwasser/abw.htm/ accessed in February 2004

Bundesverband Gas und Wasser (2003), 'Trinkwasser', www.bundesverband-gas-und-wasser.de/bgw/trinkwasser/markt-daten_x.htm/ accessed in February 2004

Cialdini, R. (1988) *Influence*, New York, Harper Collins Publishers

Dake, K. and Thompson, M. (1999) 'Making Ends Meet, in Household and on the Planet', *Innovation*, vol 12, no 3, pp427–436

Dulleck, U. and Kaufmann, S. (2004) 'Do Customer Information Programs Reduce Household Electricity Demand? – the Irish Program', *Energy Policy*, vol 32, pp1025–1032

EEA (European Environmental Agency) (2001a) 'Indicator Fact Sheet Signals 2001: Chapter Households YIR01HH06 Household Energy Consumption', http://themes.eea.eu.int/Sectors_and_activities/households/indicators/energy/ accessed in March 2004

EEA (European Environmental Agency) (2001b) 'Indicator Fact Sheet Signals 2001: Chapter Households YIR01HH08 Penetration of Environmentally Friendly Products', http://themes.eea.eu.int/Sectors_and_activities/households/indicators/eco_la bel/hh08eco_products.pdf/ accessed in March 2004

European Commission, Information and Communication Unit, Directorate-General for Research (2002) 'Eurobarometer. Energy: Issues, Options and Technologies. Science and Society', Report produced by The European Opinion Research Group (EORG) http://europa.eu.int/comm/public_opinion/archives/ebs/ebs_169.pdf/ accessed in March 2004

Eurostat (2004) http://europa.eu.int/comm/eurostat/newcronos/ accessed in January 2004

Eustat (2004) 'Estadística de Movimientos Migratorios 2001 (Análisis de resultados)', www.eustat.es/estad/temalista.asp?tema=30 &tipo=3&opt=0&mas=&idioma=c&otro=/ accessed in April 2004

Gatersleben, B., Steg, L. & Vlek, C. (2002). 'Measurement and determinants of environmentally significant consumer behavior' *Environment and Behavior,* 24 (3), pp335–362.

Halme, M. and Anttonen M. (2004) 'Sustainable Homeservice Report for Finland', www.sustainable-homeservices.com/scifi-bg-set.html/

Hertwich, E. and Katzmayr, M. (2004) *Examples of Sustainable Consumption: Review, Classification and Analysis,* NTNU, Program for Industriell Økologie, Report no 5

Hohm, D. and Wendtland, M. (2004) 'Mieterbarometer', in Scharp, M. and Jonuschat, H. (eds.) *Service Engineering*, Berlin, IZT

Housing Statistics in the European Union 2001, compiled by Dol, C. and Haffner, M., OTB Research Institute for Housing, Urban and Mobility Study, Delft University of Technology

Housing Statistics in the European Union 2002, compiled by Sak, B. and Raponi, M. International Centre for Research and Information on the Public and Cooperative Economy (CIRIEC), University of Liège

Industrie- und Handelskammer Berlin (2002) 'Berliner Wirtschaft', www.berlin.ihk24.de/share/bw_archiv/bw2002/0211021.htm./ accessed in June 2004

Instituto Nacional de Estatística (INE) (2002) Inquérito aos Orçamentos Familiares 2000 – Principais resultados, Lisboa, INE

Jasch, C., Hrauda, G. and Puhrer J. (2004) 'Sustainable Homeservices – Country Report for Austria', www.sustainable-homeservices.com/scifi-bg-set.html/

Jonuschat, H. and Scharp, M. (2004) 'German Sustainable Homeservice Report', www.sustainable-homeservices.com/scifi-bg-set.html/

Kortman, J., Derijcke, E., Gijswijt, J. and Otto, A. (2004) 'Sustainable Homeservices – Country Report for the Netherlands', www.sustainable-homeservices.com/scifi-bg-set.html/

Mejkamp, R. (2002) *Changing Consumer Behaviour through Eco-efficient Services: An Empirical Study on Car-sharing in the Netherlands,* Delft, Delft University of Technology, Design for Sustainability Reseach Programme, publication no. 3

Mont, O. (2004) 'Institutionalisation of Sustainable Consumption Patterns Based on Shared Use', *Ecological Economics*, vol 50, pp135–153

Mont, O. and Plepys, A. (2004) *From Ownership to Service-based Lifestyles: The Case of Joint Use of Power Tools and Shared Computer Resources,* Final Report to the Society for Non-Traditional Technology, Japan, Lund University, February 20

Serrano, R. and Velte, D. (2004) 'Sustainable Homeservices – Country Report for Spain', www.sustainable-homeservices.com/scifi-bg-set.html/

Thøgersen, J. and Ölander, F. (2003) 'Spillover of Environment-friendly Consumer Behaviour', *Journal of Environmental Psycho logy*, vol 23, pp225–236

Trindade, P., Duarte, P., Rocha, C., Fernandes, R. and Camocho, D. (2004) 'Sustainable Homeservices – Country Report for Portugal', www.sustainable-homeservices.com/scifi-bg-set.html/

United Nations (2003) Water for People. Water for Life – The World Water Development Report (WWDR), http://portal.unesco.org/en/ev.php-URL_ID=10064&URL_DO=DO_TOPIC&URL_SECTION=201.html accessed in March 2004.

Chapter 4

Halme, M. and Anttonen M. (2004) 'Sustainable Homeservice Report for Finland', www.sustainable-homeservices.com/scifi-bg-set.html/

Hohm, D., Hoppe, A., Jonuschat, H., Scharp, M., Scheer, D. and Scholl, G. (2002) *Dienstleistungen in der Wohnungwirtschaft: Professionelle Entwicklund neuer Serviceangebote,* Dokumentation des Workshops, Berlin, Institut für ökologische Wirtschaftsforschung (IÖW) gGmbH, November 11

Housing Statistics in the European Union 2002, Compiled by Sak, B. and Raponi, M. International Centre for Research and Information on the Public and Cooperative Economy (CIRIEC), University of Liège

Jasch, C., Hrauda, G. and Puhrer J. (2004) 'Sustainable Homeservices – Country Report for Austria, www.sustainable-homeservices.com/scifi-bg-set.html/

Jonuschat, H. and Scharp, M. (2004) 'German Sustainable Homeservice Report', www.sustainable-homeservices.com/scifi-bg-set.html/

Kortman, J., Derijcke, E., Gijswijt, J. and Otto, A. (2004) 'Sustainable Homeservices – Country Report for the Netherlands', www.sustainable-homeservices.com/scifi-/

Serrano, R. and Velte, D. (2004) 'Sustainable Homeservices – Country Report for Spain', www.sustainable-homeservices.com/scifi-bg-set.html/

Statistics Finland (2001) Helsinki, Business Register 2001

Tischner, U. and Verkuijl, M. (2002) 'SusProNet Report: First Draft Report of PSS review', www.suspronet.org/fs_reports.htm, accessed in June 2005

Trindade, P., Duarte, P., Rocha, C., Fernandes, R. and Camocho, D. (2004) 'Sustainable Homeservices – Country Report for Portugal', www.sustainable-homeservices.com/scifi-bg-set.html/

Vercalsteren, A. and Gerken, T. (2004) 'Suspronet Report WP11: Need Area Households', August, www.suspronet.org/fs_reports.htm, accessed in September 2004

Chapter 5

Ahlqvist, Heiskanen, Kallio (2005) Tulevaisuuden Kuluttajien Elämäntavat ja Ekotehokkaiden Innovaatioiden Hyväksyttävyys – Case Senioritaloihin Muuttavat Ikääntyvät (Lifestyles of Future Consumers and Acceptability of Eco-efficient Innovations – Case Elderly Moving to Senior Houses), Helsinki, National Consumer Research Centre, Työselosteita ja esitelmiä 92

CEFEC (Confederation of European Social Firms, Employment Initiatives and Co-operatives) (2005). www.cefec.de./ accessed in April 2005

DiMaggio, P. and Powell, W. (1991) 'The Iron Cage Revisited: Institutional Isomorphism and Collective Rationality in the Organizational Fields', in Powell, W. and DiMaggio, P. (eds.) The New Institutional and Organizational Analysis, Chicago, University of Chicago Press

Eurostat (2004) http://europa.eu.int/comm/eurostat/newcronos/ accessed in January 2004

Finnish Tax Administration (2005) 'Kotitalousvähennys' (Household tax deduction), www.vero.fi/nc/doc/download.asp?id=3988;60337/ accessed in April 2005

German Income Tax Law § 35a

Halme, M. and Anttonen M. (2004) 'Sustainable Homeservice Report for Finland', www.sustainable-homeservices.com/scifi-bg-set.html/

Hrauda, G., Jasch. C., Kranzl, S. and Horvath, F. (2002) Homeservices aus der Fabrik der Zukunft. Endbericht, Eigenverlag des IÖW Wien, Schriftenreihe 30/02. Available also at www.ioew.at/ioew/download/Endbericht_homeservice.pdf/

Jasch, C., Hrauda, G. and Puhrer J. (2004) 'Sustainable Homeservices – Country Report for Austria, www.sustainable-homeservices.com/scifi-bg-set.html/

Jonuschat, H. and Scharp, M. (2004) 'German Sustainable Homeservice Report', www.sustainable-homeservices.com/scifi-bg-set.html/

Kortman, J., Derijcke, E., Gijswijt, J. and Otto, A. (2004) 'Sustainable Homeservices – Country Report for the Netherlands', www.sustainable-homeservices.com/scifi-/

Niilola, K., Valtakari, M. and Kuosa, I. (2005) 'Kysyntälähtöinen Työllistäminen ja Kotitalousvähennys', (Demand-based employment and household tax reduction), Ministry of Labour, Labour policy research, no. 226

Ministry of the Environment (2002) 'Asuinkiinteistöjen energiansäästö tehostuu' (Energy saving of dwelling will become more efficient), Notice of the Ministry of Environment, November 6, www.ymparisto.fi, accessed in March 2004

Varjonen, J., Aalto, K. and Leskinen, J. (2005) Homeservice Markets, (in Finnish), Helsinki, Sitra

Chapter 6

Bowers, M.R. (1985) An Exploration into New Service Development, Structure and Organization, College Station, Texas A&M University

DIN Deutsches Institut für Normung (1998) Service Engineering – Entwicklungsbegleitende Normung für Dienstleistungen, Berlin, DIN Fachbericht no 75

Hohm, D., Jonuschat, H., Scharp, M., Scheer, D., Scholl, G. (2004) *Innovative Dienstleistungen „Rund um das Wohnen" Professionell Entwickelt*, Berlin, GdW Bundesverband deutscher Wohnungsunternehmen

Jonuschat, H. and Scharp, M. (2004) 'German Sustainable Homeservice Report', www.sustainable-homeservices.com/scifi-bg-set.html/

Kano, N., Seraku, N., Takahashi, F. and Tsuji, S. (1996) 'Attractive Quality and Must-be Quality', in Hromi, J.D. (eds.) *The Best on Quality,* Milwaukee, vol 7 of the BookSeries of the International Academy for Quality

Mandelbaum, A. (1999) Service Engineering. Modelling, Analysis and Inference of Stochastic Service Networks, project report, Haifa, Israel Institute of Technology

Normann, R. and Ramirez, R. (1994) *'Designing Interactive Strategy: From Value Chain to Value Constellation'*, Chichester, John Wiley and Sons

Ramaswamy, R. (1996): Design and Management of Service Processes. Boston, Reading

Räsänen, K. (1994) *'Kehittyvä Liiketoiminta'* [Business in Development], Porvoo, Weilin+Göös

Van Sambeek, P. and Kampers, E. 2004 *'NU-Spaarpas'*, Rotterdam, Stichting Points

Tempelman, E. (ed.) (2004) 'SusProNet Report. PSS for Need Area Food: An Overview' www.suspronet.org/fs_reports.htm, accessed in June 2005

Timmers, P. (1999) *'Electronic Commerce. Strategies and Models for Business-to-Business Trading'*, West Sussex, John Wiley and Sons

Tischner, U. and Verkuijl, M. (2002) 'SusProNet Report: First Draft Report of PSS review', www.suspronet.org/fs_reports.htm, accessed in June 2005

Tukker, A. and van Halen, C. (2003) 'Innovation Scan for Product Service Systems', www.suspronet.org/, accessed in June 2005

Vercalsteren, A. and Gerken, T. (2004) 'Suspronet Report WP11: Need Area Households', August, www.suspronet.org/fs_reports.htm, accessed in September 2004

Chapter 7

Layard, R. (2005) 'Happiness: Lessons from a New Science', London, Allen Lane

Hamilton, C. (2003) 'Growth Fetish'. Crows Nest, Allen & Unwin

Index
